X294633579

YASIR ARAFAT

A Life of War and Peace

ELIZABETH FERBER

THE MILLBROOK PRESS
BROOKFIELD, CONNECTICUT

Cover photograph courtesy of The Bettmann Archive
Photographs courtesy of Liaison International: pp. 12 (© Georges
Merillon), 112 (© Nabil), 115 (© Cyril Le Tourneur); The Bettmann
Archive: p. 20; Giraudon/Art Resource: p. 23; UPI/Bettmann:
pp. 33, 39, 41, 57, 62, 70, 75, 83, 86, 95, 122, 128; AP/Wide World:
pp. 36, 46; Sygma: pp. 97 (© M. Philippot), 105 (© M. Milner).
Map by Frank Senyk.

Library of Congress Cataloging-in-Publication Data
Ferber, Elizabeth, 1967.
Yasir Arafat : a life of war and peace / Elizabeth Ferber.
p. cm.
Includes bibliographical references (p.   ) and index.
Summary: A biography of PLO chairman Yasir Arafat
that combines the story of his life with
that of the Arab-Israeli battle over Palestine.
ISBN 1-56294-585-8 (lib. bdg.)
1. Arafat, Yasir, 1929–   —Juvenile literature.   2. Palestinian
Arabs—Biography—Juvenile literature.   3. Munaẓẓamat al-Taḥrīr al-
Filasṭīnīyah—Biography—Juvenile literature.   4. Jewish-Arab
relations—1949—Juvenile literature.   5. Israel-Arab conflicts—
Juvenile literature.   [1. Arafat, Yasir, 1929–   .   2. Palestinian
Arabs.   3. Jewish-Arab relations—1949]   I. Title
DS119.7.A6785F47   1995   956.04'092—dc20   [B]   94-48285   CIP   AC

Note About Spelling

Yasir Arafat's name generally appears in print in one of three ways: Yasir, Yasser, or Yaser. I have chosen *Yasir* as the spelling for this biography because it is the one most frequently used in newspapers, magazines, and other books.

Words such as Muslim and Moslem can be spelled either way. I have chosen *Muslim* here.

Contents

————■————

In my line of work,
you never stop, and you never give up hope.

YASIR ARAFAT

Chapter One

A Tenuous Peace

THE QUESTION on everyone's mind and what the three thousand witnesses were wondering as they sat in the bright fall sunshine on the South Lawn of the White House in Washington, D.C., was how the two aging soldiers and sworn enemies would react to being on the same dais together. When Yasir Arafat, chairman of the Palestine Liberation Organization, and Yitzhak Rabin, prime minister of Israel, signed their respective copies of a peace agreement on September 13, 1993, they took the first tangible step ever toward peace between Jews and Palestinians.

Even though they did not declare a mandate to end all of their conflicts, the two veterans of many bloody and brutal battles in the Middle East had taken part in a historic event most thought would never take place. Moments later, cradled in the outstretched arms of United States president Bill Clinton, the two men sealed their agreement with a historic handshake. The audience, which included

PLO chairman Yasir Arafat and Prime Minister Yitzhak Rabin are framed by U.S. president Bill Clinton's outstretched arms as they seal the historic Middle East peace agreement with a handshake. September 13, 1993.

former presidents Jimmy Carter and George Bush, let out a hopeful sigh.

Arafat had been banished from the United States for nearly two decades and was clearly thrilled to be treated as a foreign dignitary during his arrival at Andrews Air Force Base outside of Washington. Before he was whisked away in a black limousine to the ANA Westin hotel, Arafat told reporters, "We are very happy to come in this historic moment when we can make peace, a real peace."[1] To many of the Palestinian Americans who flocked to Washington hoping to catch a glimpse of the PLO leader, the peace summit suggested hopes for a future without violence, desolation, and rage for Palestinians and Israelis.

Few who had been involved in the planning of the summit since its conception in Madrid, Spain, in 1991 could have envisioned that Arafat and Rabin would have actually come to the meeting, much less shaken hands. The millions of viewers watching on television could hardly believe it either. But after months of covert sessions in Europe with representatives from the PLO, Israel, Norway, the United States, and several other nations, there they were, making an overt gesture for change.

While eminent heads of states from as far away as Russia and Tunisia heralded the signing of the *Declaration of Principles* as a chance for Jews and Palestinians to live together in peace and share the Holy Land along the Jordan River that both call home, many factors hindered the actuality of a workable settlement in the near or distant future.

For a host of reasons, Palestinians and Jews have fought over the right to live on the small piece of land nestled between Egypt, Jordan, and Lebanon. The Jews and Arabs have waged war on each other since 1947 when the United Nations divided Palestine between the Jews living there and the Palestinians, who were also living under British rule. The Palestinians believed the land should never have been partitioned and that the Jews had no right to be there. The Jews claimed Israel as their biblical homeland and refused to leave.

For many years, Arafat was considered the sole representative for the Palestinian people. He has been chairman of the PLO since 1969. Since the peace agreement of 1993, the only official state the Palestinians could claim was the heavily populated, narrow and dusty Gaza Strip and the town of Jericho. Many continued to live in poverty and destitution as refugees in other Arab countries and the occupied territories of Israel, where violence and death on both sides were daily occurrences.

While Arafat has been credited for bringing the Palestinian cry for statehood and autonomy into the international spotlight, he was also reviled as a violent terrorist and self-professed enemy of the Jews. Many people thought it ironic that he received the Nobel Peace Prize in October 1994 because of his past—and perhaps ongoing—terrorist activities. Some viewed him as a freedom-fighting, gun-slinging revolutionary, while others claimed he was an opportunist and a murderer.

Despite media focus, Arafat remained a surprisingly private individual, generally refusing in interviews to discuss his personal life. He also escaped many assassination attempts, leading some to believe he had "nine lives."

A follower of Islam, Arafat, whose mother traced her lineage back to the Prophet Mohammed, was born at a time of great disruption and change. From early childhood, he was trained to fight an enemy, and from the start he committed his life to this task. It was remarkable that the man who had sworn, at one point, to destroy Israel by whatever means necessary, would come to say: "The battle for peace is the most difficult battle of our lives. It deserves our utmost efforts because the land of peace, the land of peace yearns for a just and comprehensive peace."[2]

Arafat's views about Jews and his homeland were in many ways formed by his father's powerful influence when he was a child. Only after years of war and hardship did Arafat's beliefs about his embroiled homeland become more moderate. It is difficult to say exactly what prompted his change of heart. By supporting Iraq and Saddam Hussein during the Persian Gulf War of 1991, the oil-rich countries of Kuwait and Saudi Arabia, which had each given the PLO billions of dollars since 1969, were so angered that they refused to give any more money. The PLO was brought to the brink of financial ruin. Perhaps Arafat was playing the role of the wheeling and dealing diplomat in order to secure funds for his nearly bankrupt organization from outside the Arab world. Others believed he enjoyed wearing the hat of statesman and meeting with foreign dignitaries, speaking at the White House, and being hosted abroad.

At home, however, Arafat was contending with a growing number of factions within the PLO. He angered many extremists by conceding anything to Israel, even by simply agreeing to acknowledge its right to exist. There were complicated religious, political, and historical reasons why so many of Arafat's fellow Palestinians felt that he had abandoned them and that they needed a new voice to represent their needs. But no legitimate or powerful figure emerged to challenge Arafat's authority. While grassroots militant organizations, such as those engaged in the *Intifada*—meaning "uprising"—garnered media attention and presented the problems in the occupied territories, their true effect on Palestinian progress was limited.

Arafat has always felt it unnecessary to answer to others for his actions. He made no attempt to justify his marriage to Suha Tawil, for instance, a graduate of the Sorbonne in Paris, a Christian, and a woman thirty-four years his junior. If he chose to change his mind in regard to Palestine, too, that was his decision. He had spent most of his life as a militant advocate for the Palestinians, his people, but in later life he softened his militancy and worked toward peace, however tenuous. Some have continued to support him unconditionally, while others have wished him dead. Clearly, however, his central role in one of the most critical geopolitical issues of his time, the Arab-Israeli conflict, could not be denied.

Chapter Two
A Turbulent Beginning

Yasir Arafat was born on August 24, 1929, at a time when his entire culture was undergoing enormous change. The actual site of his birth has remained a mystery. Arafat has claimed he was born in a small house in the holy city of Jerusalem, currently located in the state of Israel. At the time, Jerusalem was part of British-ruled Palestine, and Arafat's ancestral home. According to Arafat, the Israelis have long since destroyed the house. Many believe that he was actually born in Cairo, where his merchant father, Abdul Rauf al-Qudwa, had moved the family.

While in Palestine, Arafat's father had run a very successful mercantile business, and his customers had included many Jews. These Jews were among the many who had been emigrating to Palestine from Europe since the late 1800s. They also claimed Palestine as their home. Palestine was the home of the Jewish religion and where the Hebrew kingdom had flourished until A.D. 70, when occupying Romans destroyed the sacred Temple in Jerusalem. Most Jews were forced to leave their Holy Land. Since that time, Jews had been living in the "diaspora," or place outside of the Holy Land, but they had always prayed to return to their homeland. They had lived for centuries in countries around the world, mostly in Europe, often persecuted and driven from place to place.

In the late nineteenth century, about five million Jews, nearly two thirds of the world's Jewish population, lived in Russia. Russian Jews suffered increasing discrimination under anti-Semitic (anti-Jewish) programs encouraged by the government. Many were slaughtered in "pogroms," which were anti-Jewish massacres. Others lost all their property and were denied employment. Between 1881 and 1920 about two and a half million Jews had to leave Russia because of economic hardship and pogroms.[1]

OTTOMAN TURKS had conquered Palestine in 1516 and ruled there until the British defeated them in World War I and took control. Inspired by European national liberation movements at the end of the nineteenth century, Jews began petitioning for a homeland and appealed to the British for help. In 1917, the same year in which Arafat's parents were married, the British Balfour Declaration was issued to support a Jewish homeland in Palestine. (The name derives from Lord Arthur James Balfour, the British foreign secretary between 1916 and 1919.) The Jews who wanted to establish a homeland embraced a political movement created in the late nineteenth century called Zionism. (Zion, a Hebrew word, was one name for the ancient homeland to which many Jews wanted to return.)

While Britain ruled Palestine, its leaders promised both the Palestinians independence and the Jews their homeland. In his book *The Arab-Israeli Conflict,* Paul Harper states: "The Arabs believed Britain had pledged itself to grant them independence, the Zionists that Britain had promised to help establish a Jewish state—both in the same piece of land. There was no way both promises could be fulfilled at the same time."[2]

As more and more Jews began to arrive in Palestine, inevitable tensions arose between the native Arabs and the immigrants. The new waves of immigrants to Palestine were politically minded, secular, and militant.

A few were inspired by a Zionist leader named Vladimir Jabotinsky, who called for the use of force against Arabs in Palestine. His intent was to establish a Jewish majority in the Holy Land. Arabs became increasingly angry as Jewish settlers bought up farmland and began building towns and cities. Although many Arabs deemed the land they sold worthless, they nevertheless resented the increasing numbers of Jews who were moving into Palestine.

Violent clashes became more and more common between Arabs and Jews. In 1921 in the city of Jaffa, the main port of entry for many immigrants, anti-Jewish riots broke out, leaving 200 Jews and 120 Arabs dead and wounded. A militia called the *Haganah* (Hebrew for "defense") was established to protect the Jewish settlements. In 1929, the year Yasir Arafat was born, there were more than over 150,000 Jews living in Palestine. Widespread fighting became commonplace throughout Palestine, especially after a violent clash broke out at the central Jewish and Muslim shrine in Jerusalem, the Western Wall.

*Jerusalem lies at the center of both the Islamic
and Judaic religions. And from this holiest of cities
rises the Western Wall, a remnant of the last Hebrew
Temple, sacred to both Jews and Muslims. Many
people have died defending their right to pray
near these ancient testaments to faith.*

In 1936 several Arab groups in Palestine joined together to form an Arab Higher Committee to protest further Jewish immigration. It called for a general strike of all workers, which grew into a rebellion against both Zionist and British authorities. In 1937 a British commission under Lord Peel recommended the partition of Palestine into separate Arab and Jewish states. The Arabs fiercely rejected this plan, and the violence intensified, causing the British to increase their military efforts in the area. It took eighteen more months to regain control of Palestine, by which time 101 British soldiers, 463 Jews, and an estimated 5,000 Arabs had been killed. With World War II looming in Europe, Britain could not afford to commit more troops to Palestine, nor did it want to offend other Arab countries for fear that they might side with Germany.

After an attempt to bring Jewish and Arab leaders together in London in 1939, Britain issued a government policy statement, known as the White Paper, which said it had no intention of making Palestine a Jewish state. The Paper called for a halt to Jewish immigration within five years and independent rule for Palestine within ten years. The Zionists once again felt betrayed. It was during these tense and historically momentous times that Arafat grew up.

ARAFAT'S MOTHER, Hamida Khalifa al-Husayni, traced her ancestry back through her father to Fatima, the daughter of the Prophet Mohammed. Like the vast majority of people in the Middle East, Arafat's family were Muslims. Their religion, called Islam— an Arabic word meaning "submission to God"—was founded by the Prophet Mohammed in the seventh century A.D. Mohammed believed he was selected by God, or Allah, as the last of the great prophets after Jesus Christ. His mission was to bring the holy word of God to the Arabs and the rest of the world. His message was that there is only one God, Allah, and that man must submit to Him.

After Mohammed's death his followers spread Islamic beliefs and practices with great success. Most of the tribes of the Arabian Peninsula adopted Islam during the seventh century. During this century these Arabs conquered the Middle East—including Palestine—and North Africa, converting the native people there to Islam.

Islam has remained an influential and widespread religion due in large part to its most sacred book, the Koran. The Koran was written after Mohammed's death and, according to Islamic belief, contained the revelations of God to Mohammed via the angel Gabriel. Through the Koran, Mohammed shared Allah's words with Muslims. The book was written in Arabic by the prophet's secretary and has always been read in this language by practicing Muslims, no matter what their native tongues.

The Koran states that there are five duties all Muslims must perform. The first is to say that "there is no God but Allah and Mohammed is his prophet." The second is to pray five times a day, each time facing Mecca, Mohammed's birthplace. The third is to give to the poor. The fourth is to fast, or go without food, during the holy month of Ramadan (the ninth month of the Muslim year), and the fifth is to make at least one pilgrimage, or religious journey, to the holy city of Mecca. These five basic demands, as well

*A miniature of a caliph, or leader, with a legion
of Islamic warriors. From the eighth to the
mid-thirteenth century, in the Golden Age of
the Arabic empire, followers of Mohammed
spread his teachings throughout the Middle East,
to North Africa and Europe, and east to India.*

as the many other Muslim codes dictating social behavior, shaped Arafat's youth and left lifelong impressions on him.

Arafat's father came from a family of wealthy merchants and traders whose ancestors had settled in the area of Palestine called Gaza. Born Rahman Abdul Rauf Arafat al-Qudwa al-Husayni, Arafat was the sixth child in his family. He was a quiet and withdrawn child, probably due in part to his mother's death from a kidney ailment when he was four years old. Afterward, he and his younger brother were sent to live with an uncle in Jerusalem for four years, during which time his father often visited them when in the city on business.

While Arafat was living in Jerusalem, his mother's relative, Haj Amin al-Husseini, was serving as the mufti, the head of Jerusalem's Muslim community. The mufti was an extreme nationalist devoted solely to the interests and culture of Arabs. He hated Jews. He inflamed Arab fears of Jewish settlement and encouraged violent acts against the immigrants. A terrorist group called the Black Hand took oaths to die for the mufti in order to preserve Arab dominance in Palestine.

Arafat lived in the city while the mufti encouraged his followers to beat up Arab landowners who sold property to Jews. In 1935, when Arafat was six years old, the mufti sponsored a Palestinian Arab party modeled along the lines of Germany's Nazi party. Then, in 1936, the mufti, as head of the Arab Higher Committee, called a general strike in Palestine to stop further Jewish immigration. The strike, which lasted eight months, brought most of the area's business to a standstill and the economy to near ruin. The mufti's violent and extremist actions and his complete unwillingness to compromise with the British and the Jews generated tremendous hatred and violence among Palestinians and outside forces. This legacy of anger weighed heavily on the region during the decades to come.

Abdul Rauf al-Qudwa married a second time when Arafat was eight and moved the boys back to Cairo. Arafat and the other children hated their new stepmother, and very soon his father divorced her, but she had left a deep impression on the young boy. For many years, he profoundly disliked women. After his father's third marriage, Arafat was primarily cared for by his oldest sister, Inam, who found him a difficult child to control. Inam did her best with her stubborn and withdrawn younger brother, but he generally ignored her. Inam made sure to walk her charge to school each morning, afraid he wouldn't go if she didn't take him there herself. According to her reports, Arafat was so quiet and antisocial that some people thought he might be mentally handicapped.

While Arafat spent a great deal of his childhood in Islamic religious study and training, the Arab-Israeli conflict was a large part of his everyday life. His immediate environment, his homelife, and the places where he played reverberated with the clashes between Arabs and Jews over the Holy Land.[3] Arafat and his brothers received their religious training primarily from their mother's uncle, Yusuf Awad al-Akbar. Akbar discovered that Arafat learned very quickly and could repeat entire passages from the Koran after seeing them only once. Arafat's teacher interpreted his intelligence and remarkable memory as signs from Allah that the young scholar was destined for greatness. Akbar tried to convince his student's father that because of these gifts, the family must treat the boy with the utmost respect.

Arafat was eager to learn from the man who treated him so well. He stayed long after regular class hours and listened intently to his uncle's lessons about Islam. Uncle Akbar was very proud of his family's connection to the Prophet Mohammed and believed his side of the family to be superior to Arafat's paternal side. Traditionally, Arab fathers have little to do with their sons' upbringing until adolescence. As a result, Arafat did not know his father very well as a child and was rather distant from him. Confident that he was marked for glory by Allah, Arafat became very difficult at home. He showed open contempt for his father and disobeyed him. Abdul Rauf al-Qudwa beat his arrogant and sullen son, but the boy remained disobedient and proud. Between the death of his mother and the nearly total absence of his father, Arafat's early years were formed by the assortment of siblings and relatives who took care of him.

Akbar received Arafat's loyalty, and the uncle found it easy to criticize the boy's father in front of Arafat and his brothers. According to one report, given by Arafat's brother Zaeed, one time their father went to Akbar and swore to kill him if he didn't stop lying to his sons. An enormous family fight exploded after Arafat refused to obey his oldest brother, whom his father had left in charge, and fled to his uncle's house. His father found him there, clinging to Akbar's robes and pleading to live with the old uncle.

At the time, Arafat's father was involved in the growing movement against Jewish settlement in Palestine and paid very little attention to family matters.

Jewish communities were flourishing, and Jews were enjoying a better standard of living than their Palestinian counterparts. While traveling on business to Cairo, Gaza, and Jerusalem, Arafat's father witnessed many conflicts between Arabs and Jews. When he returned home, he told stories of the violence and often proclaimed that the Jews were stealing Palestinian land from the Arabs.[4] Although Arafat remained distant from his father, he listened to his speeches about the Jews taking over their homeland.

Abdul Rauf al-Qudwa had joined a faction of a militant Muslim organization called the Muslim Brotherhood, which was determined to stop Jewish settlement. Abdul Rauf al-Qudwa was able to use his connections as a member of this group to have Arafat's beloved uncle Akbar killed after the family argument that caused Arafat to flee to his uncle's home in 1939. When Akbar's body was found, he had been garroted (strangled) by an iron collar and hanged, a method of execution frequently used by the Muslim Brotherhood at that time. Arafat was devastated by the death of his favorite relative, but he also learned the consequences of his father's wrath and the Brotherhood's extremism.

One of the goals of the Muslim Brotherhood, which connected Arabs in several countries, was to promote a simpler, more fundamental form of Islam by rejecting the Western influences that they felt had been plaguing the Middle East for too long. For example, strict Muslims believed and practiced that women should be entirely covered up when in public and that women should be, for the most part, confined to the home. Western beliefs encouraged women to reject these oppressive rules and seek a

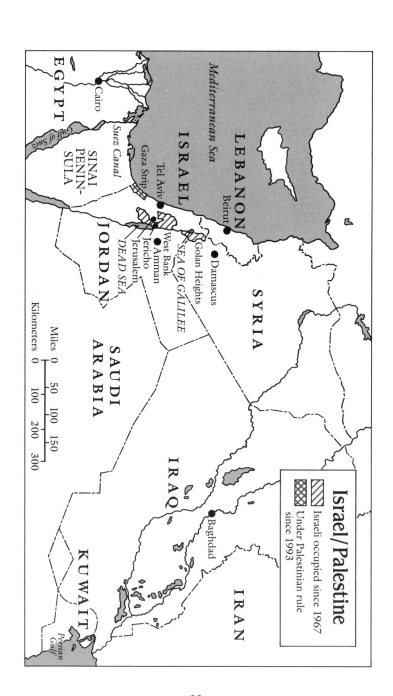

Israel/Palestine

Israeli occupied since 1967

Under Palestinian rule since 1993

more equal status in society. To fundamentalists, this was a very dangerous development because it meant not only that women were defying the Koran but that men must relinquish some of their power over them.

After the murder of Yusuf al-Akbar, Arafat's father moved the family to Gaza in Palestine to avoid questioning by the Egyptian police and to be more directly involved in the movement against the Jewish settlers. Once in Gaza, Abdul began to organize a unit of the Muslim Brotherhood that recruited young Palestinian boys into a junior guerrilla unit. He recruited a young math teacher from Lebanon named Majid Halaby to train and organize the boys, and he pledged his sons as the group's first members. It was Majid Halaby who first began to call the boy Yasir, after Yasir al-Birah, "a Palestinian who had died in the struggle against the Jews and British in Palestine."[5] The young guerrilla fighter simply transferred the devotion and admiration he had felt for his uncle Akbar to his new teacher.

Already greatly influenced by the events that conspired around him, including the deaths of his mother and his uncle, his father's harsh treatment of him, and a growing militant movement against the settlement of Jewish people in Palestine, Yasir began to prepare himself in earnest for the years of political and armed struggle ahead.

Chapter Three

Adolescent in Training

SINCE HIS UNCLE'S DEATH, Yasir had been sullen and despondent. His father hoped that membership in the young guerrilla movement would distract him. Majid Halaby was a good surrogate for Uncle Akbar and began training the young militants to see themselves as guerrillas, or *Fedayeen,* an Arabic word that means "men of sacrifice." Halaby was also involved with a group of Arab nationalists who had sent him to Gaza with secret instructions to radio intelligence information about the Middle East to a Nazi spy operation. World War II was raging in Europe at the time, and many Arabs were aiding the Nazis in Germany with hopes of shaking off the yoke of British colonial rule and stopping Jewish immigration.

In Gaza, Yasir was caught up in various plots and plans of possible heroic adventures and became even more difficult to control. He liked to roam the streets on his own rather than go to school, taking part in secret doings. At this time, Halaby began living with Yasir's family, but he soon angered Yasir's father and other parents in the community by taking a group of the young fighters to Jerusalem without their permission. The older men of the Brotherhood felt that the boys were too young and inexperienced to go on the trip and were furious at Halaby's open defiance of them.

Halaby wanted the boys to have firsthand experience in guerrilla fighting and chose Yasir to be his chief assistant. While in Jerusalem they met with a man named Abdul al-Khadir al-Husseini, the mufti's nephew and a leading guerrilla fighter. Al-Husseini told his young relative to go home and work with his father for the Arab nationalist cause.

When the group returned from Jerusalem, Halaby was killed by members of the Muslim Brotherhood. Yasir was told that Halaby had been killed in a guerrilla raid, but he remained suspicious about the true cause of his friend's death. He suspected that it was his father who had arranged the murder, just as he had been responsible for the death of another former teacher and mentor, his uncle Akbar.[1]

Yasir took Halaby's death very hard and decided soon after to devote his life to continuing his mentor's work. He was confused, however, by the many conflicting political and religious opinions of the Palestinians, who had become extremely factionalized. One thing was clear to Yasir: Palestine must be protected from Jewish and British domination. He decided to return to school in Gaza and began recruiting young militants to join the guerrilla movement in the name of his martyred teacher. Soon, he had succeeded in convincing more than three hundred young men to join the Palestinian cause.

THE BRITISH had limited Jewish immigration to Palestine in 1939. However, following World War II, news of the Holocaust increased international sympathy for them. As Jews became more determined to have a state of their own, Arab opposition and Arafat's militant feelings grew. Arafat turned sixteen in 1945, the year World War II came to an end. He was already smuggling arms from Egypt into Palestine. Due in large part to his Cairo accent, Arafat had no problem sneaking past border guards, who regularly stopped Palestinians to check for weapons.

In response to the growing strength of Arab militancy groups, Jewish groups in Palestine organized the Irgun, an extremist group whose purpose was to win Palestine by force for the Jews. Once the war in Europe ended, it became clear that the United Nations would partition Palestine and give the Jews the homeland for which they longed. Many felt they still needed strong militant groups, like the Irgun, to protect them from hostile Arabs, though. The United Nations and other peacekeeping and transition forces were nearly powerless to protect the Jews against violent attacks.

In Jerusalem and other cities fighting was intense, as both Jews and Arabs claimed this ancient place as their holy site and homeland. Determined to help in any way he could, Yasir Arafat went to Jerusalem to offer his services to the Palestinian guerrillas.

JERUSALEM HOLDS enormous religious significance for both Jews and Arabs, but for different reasons. According to the Bible, it was on Mount Moriah,

Polish boys, accompanied by a nurse, have found a safe haven in Palestine far from the horrors of the Nazi occupation. March 1943.

which later became part of Jerusalem, that Abraham, father of Judaism and an important prophet of Islam, offered to sacrifice his son Isaac to show his obedience to God. Around 960 B.C., the Jewish king Solomon built the First Temple, which was later destroyed by the Babylonians, in Jerusalem. It was here that the Second, and last, Hebrew Temple was built by King Herod in the first century B.C. Muslims believe that Jerusalem is where the Prophet Mohammed arrived from Mecca "astride his winged horse al-Buraq and here that he stopped and tied his magical animal to the wall before he ascended to heaven."[2] The only remnant of the sacred Second Temple, known as the Western Wall, is a holy site for both religions.

Jerusalem is more than a religious center. It became the capital of Palestine under British rule, as it had been in ancient times. The city flourished as a trade center, and new money poured in from abroad. Buildings were constructed, civic projects initiated, the water supply increased, and new roads installed under British organization. The city has been vitally important to both Jews and Arabs for thousands of years and remains a central issue in the Arab-Israeli conflict.

Both Arabs and Jews cited ancient claims to Palestinian land during the 1940s, the Arabs calling the area Palestine and the Jews calling it Israel. Both believed God had chosen them as heirs to the land. The area both groups claim is a strip of mostly arid land with the Mediterranean Sea bordering it to the west, Egypt's Sinai Peninsula to the southwest, and Syria and Lebanon to the north. Central to three religions—Judaism, Christianity, and Islam—to many this sacred place is not called Palestine but simply the Holy Land.[3]

Palestine was named for the Philistines, one of the peoples who lived in the region before it was conquered by the Israelites. For several hundred years, the land was an Israelite kingdom, but it was then conquered by the Assyrians, the Babylonians, and the Persians. The Romans were the next conquerors. They named the area Palestine after the Jews unsuccessfully rebelled against their rule. In the seventh century Arab armies conquered the land and converted the majority of the population to Islam. Various Muslim dynasties ruled until 1516, when the Turkish Ottoman Empire took over and controlled the area until they lost it to the British after World War I.

When World War II ended, Britain faced anger among the Arab and Jewish populations of Palestine and violence from terrorist groups on both sides. It had never been able to resolve the issue in Palestine and now had even lost its ability to control it. In 1946 when a Jewish terrorist bomb exploded in British headquarters at the King David Hotel in Jerusalem, killing eighty-eight people, Britain appealed to the United Nations for help. Eighteen-year-old Arafat, who had resolved long before to continue fighting for the Palestinian cause, arrived in Jerusalem on November 29, 1947, just as the United Nations General Assembly voted 33 to 13 to partition Palestine. Jerusalem, because of its special religious significance, was placed under international control. The UN's plan allocated 57 percent of the land to the Jews, who then formed about one third of the country's population.

The plan was immediately rejected by the Arabs, and Britain refused to enforce it. Civil war broke out

December 1946:
The Knesset Israel *was packed*
with Jewish refugees in search of a home
after surviving the Holocaust of World War II.
Britain, caught between Arab and Jewish
hostilities, refused to allow the ship to land
in Haifa Harbor, Palestine.

between the Arabs and Jews, with the Arabs at first showing signs of victory. Zionist forces soon gained the upper hand, though, and took many of the ill-prepared Arabs by surprise. Violence escalated between the Jews and Arabs, forcing the British out. On May 14, after the last British soldier had left Palestine, the Jewish state of Israel was announced.[4] With the proclamation of Israel, the only non-Muslim country in the Middle East was established. The Palestinians felt the UN's decision was arrogant and invalid. They saw it as another move by a foreign body determined to oppress and control Palestine. However, the Palestinian guerrilla groups were too disorganized to fight the resolution. As Palestinians were faced with displacement by Jews, they felt frustrated and angry that nothing could be done for them.

During this time, Arafat was spending less and less time in school and more time preparing for armed struggle with the enemy, the Zionists. He was using his ability to speak Arabic with different accents to run guns between Cairo and Jerusalem. He took part in many life-threatening missions, including one he describes in the biography *Arafat: In the Eyes of the Beholder:* "I had heard that the Zionists had sent some of their men to buy weapons left in the Western Desert, in the el-Alamein area, and I decided to go. I found some of them buying weapons and transporting them to a ship off the coast."[5] Arafat then contacted the Arab League, a group of Arab nations that had formed in 1945 to promote Arab unity, which notified the Egyptian government about the illegal sale of weapons to the Jews. Arafat claims, "I managed to stop it."[6]

When David Ben-Gurion declared Israel a state on May 14, 1948, with himself as its first prime minister, the Israelis were already fighting an undeclared civil war with the Arabs. Arafat was a college student in Cairo. By July of 1948, the fighting had grown so fierce between Arabs and Jews that Arafat's father became frightened and moved the family from Gaza back to Cairo. Several other Arab countries, agreeing with the Palestinians that there could be no compromise about the situation concerning Israel, decided to declare war immediately. The combined armed forces of Egypt, Jordan, Syria, Lebanon, and Iraq marched into Palestine to attack the Jews.

Arafat aided the invading Egyptian army by carrying supplies and water and helping in noncombat areas. Much to the Arabs' surprise and dismay, the nascent Israeli army repelled the invaders and pushed them back across their borders. When it looked as though the Palestinians were certain to be defeated, Arab support troops finally arrived, but army officials worried that local Palestinian guerrillas, of which Arafat was one, could not be kept under control. They refused to allow the Palestinians to engage in battle and took their weapons away. Arafat, who was positioned in Jerusalem for most of the war, remarked on this: "I still remember when the Arabs took the decision, and they began to prevent the Palestinians from participating. The Egyptian army took my armaments. They guarded us and took our weapons. . . . I was furious. They took our weapons and we began to feel that there was something wrong. There was a betrayal."[7]

When a truce was finally declared in January of 1949, Israel had not only won the war but also in-

*June 1948: Palestinian soldiers shell Israeli
positions in an effort to retain control of
the supply route between Tel Aviv and
Jerusalem. After the Jews declared Israel
a state in May 1948, fighting escalated.*

creased its landholdings by about half, including western Jerusalem, which was supposed to have been an international and neutral zone. Transjordan (now Jordan) was given East Jerusalem. By fighting to retain all of Palestine, Arab leaders had caused the Palestinians to lose even more land.[8] If the Palestinians had agreed to the original partition by the United Nations, hundreds of thousands of them would not have become refugees, never to return home again. A Palestinian state could still have been established out of the land not yet lost to Israel, but neighboring Arab countries claimed it for themselves and carved up the nation further. Egypt claimed the area around Gaza, known as the Gaza Strip, and Transjordan took control of the central hill region west of the Jordan River known as the West Bank. Syria took a small strategic area in the north that overlooks the town of Galilee, and Jerusalem was divided, with Israel taking one half and Transjordan the other.

By the end of the war, some 725,000 Palestinian refugees had fled their native land. Some went north to Lebanon and Syria, while others went south to Gaza and across the Jordan River to Transjordan. Many left in panic, to the sounds of Israeli voices booming over loudspeakers telling them to get their women and children out, and ended up in refugee camps where they were treated as second-class citizens in their host countries. The refugees in camps were not allowed to become citizens of the other Arab countries and were put in makeshift settings and treated as temporary refugees who would return home soon.

In 1949, nineteen-year-old Yasir Arafat was one of the few refugees who could return to his family

This brother and his younger sister were among the 725,000 Arabs who fled to refugee camps after the 1948 Israeli victory.

home in Cairo. Arafat's family, especially his father, put pressure on him to attend a university; he even applied to the University of Texas. While waiting for a visa to enter the United States, Arafat rethought his position and "saw a new way forward." He said to himself, "No, I will not leave."[9] He decided not to go to college in America but to stay in the Middle East and continue fighting for the Palestinian cause. He enrolled in a technological high school and became very proficient at building explosives. Many of the school's teachers were sympathizers or members of the Muslim Brotherhood and used the school's facilities to manufacture bombs. Arafat was pleased to be making bombs to be used against the enemy, Israel. His father meanwhile had rejoined the Brotherhood, taking a job with the mufti in Egyptian-controlled Gaza, and, once again, in 1949 moved the family back to Palestine to be more useful to the organization. In Gaza, Arafat worked with his brothers to recruit young Palestinians to fight.

Arafat also put his guerrilla training, honed in Egypt, to good use in Gaza. Many homeless and poor Palestinians favored the annexation of the West Bank by Jordan because they wanted to become Jordanian citizens. Arafat didn't agree with them and led a band of young guerrillas throughout Gaza attacking and murdering Palestinians who favored the proposal. However, despite his efforts, in 1950 the annexation of the West Bank by Jordan was complete.

Arafat was now at a loss as to how to proceed, and in 1950 he yielded to his father once again. He returned to Cairo to pursue a university education. He could not help but think, as he traveled back to Egypt, of the dispersed Palestinians who would probably never see their cities, villages, and homes again. They had very few, if any, rights in other countries, no passports, no jobs, and had lost their national as well as cultural identities. They were "homeless, stateless people wanting only to return to their Palestine. They would never allow their Arab brothers to forget their plight; they would never allow their enemy, Israel, to live in peace."[10] Yasir Arafat had begun the journey to lead the Palestinians in their fight to regain their land, and almost as important, a sense of identity as a people.

Chapter Four
Guerrilla Tactics

WHEN ARAFAT returned to Cairo, he enrolled at the modern, westernized University of Fuad the First (later Cairo University) in August 1951 to study civil engineering. As a child Arafat had always been deft at constructing such things as paper cameras and ham radios and clever at math and chess, so a course in engineering seemed the natural choice. Arafat's father wanted his son to pursue higher education, knowing that "the answer to his future lay in earning a university degree."[1] After making sure his son was secured at college, Abdul was forced to leave Egypt because he had lost a lawsuit with the government and in the process his land and money. He lived out the rest of his life in Gaza. When he died in 1954, Arafat did not attend his funeral.

Many Palestinian Arabs sought education as a means to better their positions in the world. Those Palestinians who attained a formal education often became the leading intellectuals of the Middle East, entering such professions as law, medicine, and engineering. Arafat, who was more interested in politics than engineering and science, enrolled himself in a school where the students were fervently involved in the current political situation, both in Egypt and the rest of the Middle East.

The end of World War II prompted many Arab nations to seek independence once and for all from the Western countries that had colonized them. They wanted to take charge of their own affairs, culturally, economically, religiously, and politically. Despite the differences that separated many newly formed republics in the Middle East, Arabs were united on the Israeli issue. All Arab countries wanted to see the end of Israel, but as the years passed, many found this wish less and less likely to be fulfilled.

King Abdullah of Jordan was assassinated in 1951 as he went to pray in Jerusalem, and his grandson Prince Hussein was crowned king of Jordan on his eighteenth birthday. There was a coup d'état in Syria, riots broke out in Baghdad, Iraq, and the Egyptian king, Farouk, was deposed in 1952 by a group of army officers. One particularly charismatic leader, Lieutenant-Colonel Gamal Abdel Nasser, who dedicated himself to spreading nationalism throughout the Arab world, became president of Egypt in 1956. Although he accomplished many things during his presidency, he was unable to liberate Palestine as he had promised.

As the politics of the Middle East swirled into the second half of the twentieth century, Arafat came to the forefront of the action. At home, however, Ar-

*July 1956: Newly elected Egyptian president
Gamal Abdel Nasser is greeted by wildly cheering
crowds in Cairo. Although he was successful in
creating a stronger, more coherent Arab identity,
he would fail in his ultimate goal of uniting all
Arabs under Egyptian leadership. He was
both a help and hindrance to Arafat in his
fight for the liberation of Palestine.*

afat's sister Inam was still in charge, and he shared a room with his brother Fathi, who was studying to become a doctor. Each morning, Arafat jumped the gate in front of his house and met up with his Egyptian classmates, Sami Suleiman and Kamal Naguib. The three rode to school together, walked past the main gates of the university, not far from the road that led to the ancient pyramids, and headed toward the engineering college. While Arafat tended to neglect his academic studies, he was passionately involved in politics and religion. His friend Kamal Naguib recalls, "He was always immersed in his political motivations, and you couldn't even discuss otherwise with him. It was the dream and hope of his life. He ate, drank, slept the issue—Arafat has always been a devout Muslim. He has never smoked a cigarette nor even had a glass of beer and he prayed regularly."[2]

While at college, Arafat became an important student organizer for the Muslim Brotherhood and would often disappear from campus, working as a secret volunteer for the Brotherhood. During the early 1950s the Brotherhood was responsible for a number of secret military operations against the British bases near the Suez Canal. Even though a full-scale invasion by European forces did not occur at the Suez Canal until 1956, there were many years of small-scale fighting between the occupying British forces and Arab fighters. Arafat was one of these fighters as well as a student at the university.

The university had a military training school for volunteer reserve officers that met every morning before classes, six days a week, from seven to nine. The students were drilled in shooting rifles, using machine guns, and setting mines. Arafat made sure he attended every class, and after ninety sessions plus two months of training at military camp during the summer, he was given a reserve officer's certificate. Many students enrolled in the program to avoid active military duty, but Arafat joined to gain experience and training.

In 1951, while Arafat was establishing himself as a young leader of the Palestinian cause, he met a literature student from Gaza, Salah Khalaf, who was attending an important center of Islamic studies called al-Azhar. Khalaf was a member of the Muslim Brotherhood and, after deciding to help Arafat win the presidency of the Palestinian student union, used his influence within the Brotherhood to suppress other candidates by means of violence and intimidation. Khalaf states, "I was very impressed by his obvious leadership qualities as I watched him training the students. He was very dynamic. Very tough. Very passionate."[3] As a future leader, Arafat wanted to meet each and every one of his voters. Arafat adjusted his message to suit potential voters: If there were Communists in the audience, he presented himself as a staunch believer in communism. If there were Islamic fundamentalists, he told them what they wanted to hear. His aim was to get himself into office at almost any cost.

This desire to stay in touch with the people he fights for has remained one of Arafat's trademarks. While he has not always been able to meet every group's specific interest, he has always listened to each faction and tried to understand what its members feel they need and why. He developed into a passionate and charismatic speaker who liked to know the children, widows, and soldiers of Palestine in order to better work for their, and his, cause. During the student election in 1951, which he won, Arafat also displayed another lifelong trait, that of remaining as independent as possible of any controlling organization. He has always done things his way and refused to follow anyone else's rules. This has both helped and hindered him throughout his political and military careers.

In 1952 he founded the Palestinian Student Federation (PSF), whose main goal was to work toward the destruction of Israel and the occupation of Palestine by the Palestinians. The PSF, ostensibly a cultural organization, was working under cover to unify Palestinians. "Because the infrastructure of the Palestinians had been destroyed, we had nothing," Arafat explained. "So the students' organization actually was not a union of students: it was one of the establishments for unity, identity, and support. Because we had to depend on ourselves for everything, we had to work hard, to struggle, to achieve, to get help."[4]

When Arafat took control of the organization, it was in need of leadership, focus, and motivation. Arafat convinced Egyptian authorities to let him set up a training camp for soldiers on campus, to prepare students to aid in and fight battles, such as the one with the British at the Suez Canal. He was also able to talk the Arab League—an umbrella group of Arab nations formed in 1945 to promote Arab nationalism—into giving scholarships to Palestinian students who could not afford tuition. The Egyptians were growing restless with the reign of King Farouk and his mother, Queen Nazil, and Arafat contributed to the unrest by organizing and staging marches against the government. Against a background of violence, looting, and police brutality, Egyptian president Nasser and his officers overthrew the monarchy in 1952.

Yasir Arafat's organization, the PSF, was suffering its own troubles. Internal conflicts and political differences separated group members, and in 1953 an Arafat-led faction was voted out of the group because rivals accused Arafat of favoring people from Gaza over other Palestinians. This type of factionalization within groups that Arafat associated himself with, including the Palestine Liberation Organization (PLO), have plagued him and made working toward Palestinian independence and reform endlessly frustrating for many Palestinians.

In response to his ousting, Arafat formed a new group called the General Union of Palestinian Students (GUPS) and began printing what was supposedly a student newspaper, *The Voice of Palestine*. The paper was read not only in Cairo but also in Gaza, Jordan, Syria, Iraq, and Lebanon, among other places. Thanks to the paper, which was more a manual telling scattered Palestinians how to organize than a student newspaper, GUPS membership rose dramatically. The paper encouraged exiled Palestinians to join together in small secret guerrilla units to plan raids on Israel.

Arafat wanted to unify all the Palestinian student groups in order to organize attacks against Israel. By 1953 he was a skilled and well-trained guerrilla fighter and felt confident approaching the leaders of the rival groups to promote his plans. Some resisted his efforts and were killed as a result. After the murders, carried out with the help of the Muslim Brotherhood, the PSF agreed to cooperate with Arafat, and he was elected chairman of GUPS in 1955. When Arafat left college in 1956, he had chaired student Palestinian groups for five years and honed his leadership skills. He also developed many friendships with the men who later helped him found Fatah, the armed military group that became his power base.[5]

Arafat molded his organization along the lines of a revolutionary party attempting to liberate an occupied land. He portrayed himself as the ultimate freedom fighter, sacrificing everything for his cause, Palestinian liberation. During the post-World War II 1950s, the world had divided itself into essentially two camps. In the West, there were the United States and Western Europe, politically and militarily allied, who espoused the benefits of a democratic society, with personal freedom, private property, and a free market economy. The United States also replaced Britain as the principal outside force in the Palestinian-Israeli conflict.

Allied against the West were the Soviet Union and the Warsaw Pact nations, comprising most of Eastern Europe, which were under Soviet control. The Soviet Union and most of Eastern Europe adhered to communism, which Russians adopted in their own revolution in 1917. Communism is a political ideology based on the ideas of German philosopher Karl Marx, who proposed a system whereby all property was held in common by a society. The appeal, in theory, was that there was neither a ruling class nor poverty, that everyone's basic needs were met. So far, communism has worked only in theory and not in practice, as seen by the recent disintegration and fall of the Soviet Union and most of the Warsaw Pact nations. But to the young revolutionary leader Arafat, who was going to take his people home

to Palestine and shake off the oppressive Israelis—
and indirectly Western imperialism—the Communist
system seemed the perfect path to follow.

During the 1950s, until the fall of communism,
the United States and the Soviet Union decided
whom they would aid in the Middle East and other
parts of the world based on their interests in a partic-
ular place. The United States sided with Israel, and
the Soviets decided to support the Palestinian cause.
Egyptian president Nasser began allying himself with
Communist countries in order to seek more financial
and military help. Nasser also continued to support
Arafat and other Palestinians by backing guerrilla
raids on Israel and training Palestinian fighters, including Arafat and his partners.

In addition to Salah Khalaf, Arafat formed another long-lasting friendship and partnership during
this time. Khalil al-Wazir was a Palestinian refugee
from age twelve and was training in Gaza by age
eighteen with Khalaf. Al-Wazir was arrested in Egypt
for making bombs and asked Arafat to help release
him. After Arafat succeeded, the two men met secretly in Gaza for three days and planned a raid on
Israel's water storage facilities, hoping to instigate an
Israeli declaration of war. Israel sent paratroopers into
Gaza where they hit both Palestinian and Egyptian
targets, thus exposing Egypt's military weakness. Arafat and al-Wazir tried to force Egypt into declaring
war by organizing marches, demonstrations, and riots, but the Gaza raid had humiliated Nasser, and he
did not want another defeat. At the Suez Canal he
would experience a long-awaited victory.

Nasser was known for his staunch defiance of
European powers and his nationalization of the Suez

Canal in 1956. The canal, which was built during the 1860s in Egypt by European investors and Egyptian workers, was a vital transportation link between the Mediterranean and Red seas. Oil shipments from the Middle East passed through the Suez Canal on their way to Europe. When Nasser came to power, Egypt had already obtained its independence from Britain, but the Suez Canal was still run by a French company. The crisis began after Nasser seized it from its European owners, closed the Straits of Tiran to Israeli shipping, and allowed attacks on Israeli settlements from Gaza. By closing the canal, Nasser cut off a great deal of Europe's oil supply, and the British, French, and Israeli forces decided to invade Egypt.

The invaders' plan to protect and win back control of the canal failed miserably, but there was no clear victor in the crisis. The United Nations was called in as a peacekeeping force, and the canal was closed while repairs were done. To the Arabs, however, it was a victory for Nasser and the Arab world; they had defied outside forces. Nasser was proclaimed a hero and hailed as having won this first resistance to Western imperialism. Arafat joined the Egyptian army during the crisis as part of a bomb disposal team located in Port Said. He was very shrewd to join the Suez conflict, since it gave him credentials as a soldier and allowed him to make important contacts within the Egyptian military.

Unfortunately, Nasser's glow began to pale in the eyes of many Arabs when Israeli forces devastated the Egyptian Army on the Sinai Peninsula in 1956. Again he needed more aid from the Soviet Union and began to be perceived as a Soviet threat by the United States. According to Paul Harper, "The polarization of the Arab-Israeli conflict along East-West lines quickly acquired a momentum of its own."[6] Losing against the Israelis in the Sinai gave many Arabs, who were in competition with Nasser for leadership of the Arab world, an excuse to further accuse him of incompetence and poor military leadership.

Arafat had witnessed one too many humiliating defeats by the Israelis during his association with Egypt. Disgusted, he declared that the Palestinians must fight for their own cause without interference from other "weak" Arab nations. This was a dangerous and pivotal choice for Arafat. Throughout the course of his leadership, the PLO has needed financial aid from other Arab nations; yet while he would take their money, Arafat would often refuse to do what they wanted in return for their aid. This inability to unify with other Arab countries has cost the PLO dearly in the fight against Israel.

While Arafat made his statements about wanting to distance his cause from the incompetent Egyptians, the Muslim Brotherhood reacted even more strongly and began preparing a plot to assassinate Nasser. In an attempt to appease his enemies and display Arab loyalty, Nasser united with Syria to form the United Arab Republic in 1958. The union lasted a brief three years.

Arafat was meanwhile forging his own path, making both friends and enemies in the later 1950s. In March 1957, Communist-bloc countries invited Arab student delegates from several nations to take part in an international student convention in Prague, the capital of Czechoslovakia. It was the first time the General Union of Palestinian Students was invited to an international conference of Communist youth organizations. Arafat led a delegation of eight students representing GUPS, and while they were in Prague the delegation factionalized, splitting into two groups. Five participants returned to Cairo, leaving Arafat and his two friends, Khalaf and al-Wazir, behind. The unfortunate five who returned to Egypt were immediately arrested by the secret police for their role in the Muslim Brotherhood's plot to assassinate Nasser. The students were released after questioning and sent word to the three Palestinians still in Prague not to return to Cairo.

The three friends headed instead to West Germany. Al-Wazir had cousins studying in Stuttgart, where there was a large Palestinian student population. They were safe in West Germany, but Arafat was anxious to return to the Middle East and rejoin the Palestinian cause. Looking through a German newspaper one day, Arafat noticed an ad calling for laborers to go to Kuwait, a small, oil-rich country in the Middle East on the Persian Gulf that was experiencing a growth period. The ad called for skilled workers, preferably Arabs. Arafat applied for and received an engineering position.

From the moment he arrived in 1957, Arafat enjoyed a very high standard of living in Kuwait. Palestinians made up almost 50 percent of the civil servants and 80 percent of the teachers in the tiny Persian Gulf emirate (a nation ruled by an emir, a term for government leader in the Middle East). Arafat biographers Janet and John Wallach state, "Here [Palestinians] could turn their university education into lucrative positions. Tens of thousands of Palestinians poured into the oil-rich emirate to seek their fortunes from pearls that clung to the seabeds and petroleum that oozed from the earth."[7] The sandy and arid country was an oasis of jobs and opportunity, and many of the Palestinians who worked in Kuwait were provided with housing and cars.

There wasn't much to spend their salaries on, so they sent a good part of their money to relatives living in the wretched refugee camps in Gaza, the West Bank, Lebanon, and Jordan. The Palestinians in the camps were eagerly awaiting the day they would return to their homes but were struggling to maintain their way of life in the meantime. Neighborhoods were designated, marriages arranged, and cultural activities practiced on foreign and occupied soil. Those who arrived in Kuwait during the 1950s also wanted to return home and were looking for someone to lead them.

Arafat lived in a section of Kuwait called Solaybiahat, which was designated for unmarried engineers. The strict Islamic society separated men and women for religious reasons, but it also separated workers by their occupations. His brother, Fathi, later lived in the neighborhood for doctors. Arafat initially spent his days working on public engineering projects for the Department of Water Supply, but enhanced his salary by accepting private contracts as well. He worked on the homes of many local sheiks, and it did not take him long to start his own private construction company. He hired fellow Palestinians to work for him, whom he organized into a movement to continue fighting for Palestine.

Arafat could easily have become extremely wealthy had he chosen to stay in Kuwait, as many Palestinians did, but instead he chose to remain a freedom fighter. While rich in Kuwait, Arafat did en-

*The United Nations helped build this
sprawling tent city called Nahr el Bared near
Tripoli, Lebanon. More than six thousand
Palestinians took refuge there in 1955.*

joy a few indulgences, which included a lavish trip to Venice and other European countries. He also had a passion for driving and said, "My favorite car was my Thunderbird."[8] He also boasted that he was a millionaire.

However, after a few spending sprees, Arafat used his money almost exclusively for the cause. For several years, beginning in 1957, Arafat and his companions planned the formation of a new military group. He named his nascent organization *Fatah* from a word in the Koran meaning "to open the gates for glory." He and his friends, including al-Wazir, would get together for dinner and make plans for the future, where they envisioned themselves returning gloriously to Palestine, whose gates would soon open. Arafat's group was not the only one to emerge during the late 1950s. In Syria, Saudi Arabia, Qatar, Iraq, and Gaza, other Palestinian underground groups were forming in hiding from the authorities. Many governments saw the Palestinians as a dangerous threat to their societies.

Only a few months after his own arrival, Arafat's close friend Khalil Wazir joined him in Kuwait in 1957. Then, in 1959, Salah Khalaf joined his two fellow guerrilla warriors. The three were poised to turn Fatah into a true revolutionary operation. By the fall of 1959, Arafat had raised enough money to publish a small newspaper called *Falastinuna,* or *Our Palestine.* The first issue called for an armed struggle to regain Palestinian land and inspired many who hoped to return home. The newspaper also featured stories by Palestinians arriving in Kuwait that described supposed atrocities and horrors committed by Israelis against Arabs during the 1956 war. Although Egypt and Syria banned the paper, copies were smuggled in, and Arafat's group received immediate responses from abroad in favor of the struggle. Membership in Fatah grew rapidly.

The publication was so successful that six months later, in 1960, Arafat toured Lebanese refugee camps in order to set up its distribution there. Touring the camps, Arafat could not believe the conditions in which his fellow Palestinians were living. Many camps did not have proper sanitation, electricity, plumbing, schools, hospitals, or any other facilities offering basic necessities for daily life. Arafat was so shocked that when he returned to Kuwait he was even more determined about his goal in life. He worked relentlessly to strengthen Fatah, which he hoped would bring a better way of life to all Palestinians.

Chapter Five

Emerging Leader

ARAFAT'S MAIN GOAL in the beginning of the 1960s was to present an image of himself as a true guerrilla fighter and revolutionary, one who would stop at nothing to further the cause of the Palestinian people. He also worked tirelessly to promote Fatah and win international attention for the organization. He adopted a war name—Abu Ammar—which he would also use as a code name during his clandestine entries into Israel and other Arab countries. Due to his increasing importance to the Palestinian struggle, Arafat had garnered many new friends as well as enemies and had to be extra alert and conscious of his safety at all times.

Al-Wazir, Arafat's close comrade and one of Fatah's cofounders, was working as both a teacher and the editor of *Our Palestine*. In many articles he urged readers to form small secret cells: "Just as an organic cell can split and reproduce itself, a Fatah cell could give birth to more cells in a widening network."[1] Fatah's central goal was to combine Palestinian forces everywhere in order to make them strong enough to challenge their common enemy, Israel. Because Palestinians were forbidden to form organized groups throughout the Middle East, Fatah had to work underground during its early years. When Arafat traveled to raise funds and recruit in the refugee camps, he did so secretly, letting almost no one know of his whereabouts. While there were many other underground groups working during the early 1960s, Fatah had the advantage of Arafat's and al-Wazir's organizational skills.

It was during these nascent years of Fatah that Arafat began wearing his now familiar kaffiyeh, the checkered scarf he almost always wrapped around his head. The kaffiyeh symbolized Arab nationalism and was worn during the 1930s by Arab fighters working for independence from colonial powers. The scarf also made Arafat more acceptable to Palestinian peasants, or fellahin, who viewed the kaffiyeh as a symbol that Arafat was one of them and not someone superior to them. It was one of Arafat's goals to link all Palestinians, intellectuals as well as refugees in camps, through a common identity. During the 1960s, Arafat was becoming better at finding allies who could help him increase the size and power of Fatah. Al-Wazir moved to Lebanon where he published *Our Palestine* and married his cousin Intissar. Intissar became an important supporter of Fatah and even acted as military chief while al-Wazir was in Europe buying weapons.

On July 5, 1962, Algeria declared its independence from France, and Arafat celebrated the event as a great victory for Arabs everywhere. Algeria's success

*Fatah leader Yasir Arafat (left in right photo)
inspects a newly graduated group of young
fighters. The kaffiyeh (checkered scarf), a
symbol of Arab nationalism since the 1930s,
was taken up by the Fatah and later the PLO.*

encouraged Arafat to commit all of his time to making Fatah a more powerful organization. The new Algerian government agreed to support Arafat's group, and soon Fatah's first official office, Le Bureau de la Palestine, opened in Algiers with al-Wazir as its manager. The office in Algeria gave Fatah a place to meet with other revolutionaries from all over the world, and Arafat frequently traveled there from his home in Kuwait.

Modeling themselves after the Algerian revolutionaries, Arafat and his colleagues hoped that after an armed struggle the Jews would flee Palestine much as the French had fled Algeria. However, according to Barry Rubin in his book *Revolution Until Victory: The Politics and History of the PLO,* the "tendency to overestimate Arab armed might and underestimate Israeli steadfastness would long plague both Arafat and Fatah."[2] What Arafat failed to realize throughout the 1960s was that Israel was itself fighting a battle for its right to exist and didn't consider itself a colonial power invading and overrunning someone else's land. Like the Palestinians, the Israelis felt they were finally back in their homeland. Arafat also viewed the United States as the sole reason why Israel was able to continue existing at all. His inability to understand Israel's true nature and determination would cost him dearly in lives, money, and land for years to come.

During a meeting with Chinese Communists, Arafat was offered arms if he could prove that Fatah had a history of successful commando raids against Israel. This was a greater incentive for Arafat to begin new and covert military actions against his enemy. In 1963 and 1964, Fatah set up military training bases in both Jordan and Syria to begin operations in January 1965.

In February 1963, Arafat and his closest colleagues, who included al-Wazir, Khalaf, and three other men—Qaddumi, Khalid al-Hasan, and Hani al-Hasan—formed the first central committee. This group became the foundation for the current leadership in the PLO. Many of the members wanted the organization to be led collectively, with each man holding equal amounts of influence and power, but Arafat did not agree. He felt the group could best be led with the power resting in one man's hands, his own.

As Fatah grew in strength and power, other Arab regimes worked hard to revive the Palestinian issue out of self-interest. Nations such as Iraq and Egypt wanted to control the movement so that they could reap whatever benefits might come from the situation, such as foreign aid and land grants adjoining Israel. Nasser was always interested in gaining more territory and ruled the Gaza strip with great force. Even so, he did not feel militarily strong enough to attack Israel.

At a meeting of the Arab states in January 1964, Nasser proposed establishing an organization supposedly dedicated to Palestinian self-rule, and thus the Palestine Liberation Organization was born. Nasser's choice for PLO president, a Palestinian lawyer and diplomat named Ahmad Shuqairi, was elected. So far, the formation of the PLO and the election of its first president had been all arranged by men other than those directly affected by the situation in Palestine. While Nasser proposed the formation of the PLO, leaders of other Arab states had to approve its creation. The plan backfired because the leaders did not possess a genuine concern for the Palestinian people.

As Barry Rubin relates, "Ironically, then, although the PLO would eventually struggle with Arab regimes and come to favor a West Bank/Gaza Palestinian state, it was set up precisely to oppose any such state and to be a puppet for those regimes."[3]

While some of Fatah's leaders unofficially observed the meeting, none claimed to have actually taken part. It was Shuqairi who wrote the PLO charter that was adopted on June 1, 1964. The organization's stated purpose was to liberate Palestine and destroy Israel. Soon thereafter, the Arab League agreed to create a military arm of the PLO, but the officers who controlled the army were not Palestinians.

From the very beginning, Arafat wanted complete control of Palestinian liberation, and he resisted the directives of other Arab governments. He preached that Palestinians "had to be rescued from the stranglehold of Arab tutelage, inter-party discord, and regional Arab policies."[4] He continued, "It is high time that the Palestinians should cease to be used as pawns to further personal or regional ends. The Palestinians' cause must now emerge on the international scene as a liberation struggle between the Palestinian people and an occupying state. All that we ask of the Arab governments is that they should be able to protect their own frontiers and to permit and support Palestinian action inside the occupied territories."[5] He viewed the occupied territories as Gaza, the West Bank, and Israel itself.

Arafat soon felt that his headquarters in Algeria was too far away from Palestine to offer a strong political base. He began looking for another sponsor, and in 1964 he moved his headquarters to Damascus, Syria. Arafat enlisted recruits from student organizations and refugee camps, and received money from wealthy Palestinians who were friends of Fatah's leaders. After many months of preparation and training, Arafat felt that the military unit of Fatah, al-Asifa, was ready to make an attack.

Their first attempt was the bombing of Israel's water supply on January 1, 1965. The raid was a failure, and their commander, Ahmed Musa, was killed—not by an Israeli soldier but by a Jordanian who shot him when he refused to give up his gun. The first attacks made by the organization were generally ineffective, and Israel had no difficulty defending itself. By this time, Arafat was again moving from place to place, a habit that he maintained, spending no more than two nights in the same place for safety purposes. Very few people knew where Arafat was at any given moment.

After a miserably unimpressive beginning, Fatah increased raids on Israel from Jordan during 1965 and into 1966 with Syrian support. Israel was becoming increasingly irate and started putting pressure on Jordan to stop the Palestinian attacks. When three Israeli soldiers were killed by a land mine, the Israeli army attacked the Jordanian village of Samua and killed several Palestinians. They also raided Palestinian military camps on the West Bank, displaying a hint of the offensive might that would make them an unbeatable force to contend with in the future.

Arafat was also having problems in Syria after a coup d'état in 1966 replaced his main supporter. The Syrians now wanted to replace Arafat with a Syrian officer and plotted his removal as Fatah's leader. The Syrian officer was soon found dead. Although the exact circumstances of his murder and who killed him remained a mystery, the Syrians blamed Arafat. Arafat and Fatah's core leadership were jailed and told they would be released if they confessed to the slaying. Eventually they were released without confessing, and Arafat reacted by forming an alliance with Egypt. In response, Syria and Iraq established separate Palestinian groups to act in their own interests. Syria, Iraq, and other Arab states sought control over the same area for which the Palestinians and the Israelis fought so desperately. There were untold economic, political, and military advantages for various Arab countries if they could establish power in the small piece of land that had become Israel.

Syria's new regime was much more radical than the former one and provoked border clashes with Israel that raised tensions throughout the Arab nations. Israel was particularly upset that almost all the attacks were against innocent civilians—farmers, children, and border residents. One report during the spring of 1967 relates that on the morning of April 7,

> Syrian troops opened fire on an unarmed tractor ploughing fields near a northern Israeli settlement. The Israeli military retaliated swiftly. By early that afternoon, the air force was deployed, and while Syrian citizens watched, Israeli Mirages destroyed six Soviet-supplied MIG fighter planes in the air, two of them near Damascus. By five o'clock Syrian airplanes had disappeared from the sky and five Israeli tractors were back out ploughing the border fields.[6]

IN MAY 1967, the Soviet Union spread rumors through its extensive intelligence network that Israel was planning an attack on Syria, and in response, Syria, Jordan, Iraq, and Egypt formed a military alliance. Egyptian president Nasser requested that United Nations peacekeeping forces be removed from the Sinai Peninsula, which the UN secretary-general agreed to do. Nasser quickly moved 80,000 Egyptian troops to the Peninsula and stopped Israeli shipping through the Straits of Tiran by closing the port of Eilat. Israel prepared itself for war.

As Arab forces were preparing for a war with their common enemy, Israel decided to make the first move. On Monday morning June 5, 1967, the Israeli air force struck Egyptian air bases from the Suez Canal to Cairo and within a few hours had destroyed the Egyptian air force. In response, Iraq and Syria dropped bombs on Israel, which did very little damage. The Israelis then turned their attention to wiping out all of the Jordanian and nearly half of the Syrian air forces. The ground fighting was equally as impressive and one-sided, with the Israeli army wiping out the combined forces of Egypt, Syria, Iraq, and Jordan in six days.

The victors captured the Sinai Peninsula from Egypt and once again the militarily strategic Golan Heights overlooking Galilee from Syria. They also rid the area west of the Jordan River, the West Bank, of Jordanian troops. The Israelis could now claim both the western and eastern parts of Jerusalem as their own. On June 5, Fatah's military commander, al-Wazir, was in Germany buying arms. When he returned home, he and Arafat immediately set off for the front. But by the time they reached the Golan Heights, Syrian troops were already retreating. Yasir Arafat, "who had driven to the Syrian front in his Volkswagen car, never even got to fight."[7]

On June 8, the Egyptians surrendered, followed soon after by the Syrians, who waved the white flag in the Golan Heights on June 10. Israel had virtually destroyed the enemy, who less than a week earlier had sworn to drive it into the sea. Instead, Israel now occupied an area four times its original size. The war also created 200,000 more Palestinian refugees who had fled to the East Bank of Jordan and left a million and a half Arabs living in lands occupied by Israel. The war served to highlight the incompetence and disorganization of the Arab forces while at the same time demonstrating Israel's military superiority.

Israel did offer the West Bank and the Gaza Strip back to the Arabs in exchange for peace and Arab recognition of Israel's right to exist. The Arab leaders once again failed to accept an offer of land for peace and told Israel there would be no peace, no negotiations, and no recognition of Israel. While the various humiliated Arab governments planned to fight again in the future, the Palestinians who had lost their homes and their land during the war were left in limbo. They were the greatest losers in the Six Day War.

Shortly after the war, Fatah's leaders met in Damascus, Syria, to discuss their next move. Some wanted to give up the struggle and try to establish lives in other Arab countries. Arafat refused to quit and argued that Israeli occupation of Gaza and the West Bank would only serve to unite the Palestinians there even more. Arafat believed that it was time to set up Fatah operations in Palestine itself, specifically in the occupied territories. Not everyone stood behind Arafat, afraid that once he took control of the group, he would turn into a virtual dictator and abuse his position. When Arafat himself was nearly at the

*June 1967: Victorious Israeli soldiers
pray at Jerusalem's ancient Western Wall
at the end of the Six Day War.*

point of defeat, good news came from Hani al-Hassan.

Al-Hassan reported that hundreds of Palestinian students had left schools in Europe when the Six Day War began and were now training in guerrilla tactics in Algeria. They would arrive in the occupied territories in a matter of days. With renewed hope, Fatah members rallied around Arafat and were ready to resume the fight for the homeland. Fatah began a propaganda campaign in order to lift the damaged morale of the Palestinians. Leaders toured refugee camps urging people to train as terrorists and make raids into Israel.

Fatah was able to secure funds from other Arab governments for arms and supplies, and the newly trained student commandos arriving from Algeria and China were ready to fight. As the new terrorists infiltrated the occupied areas, Israeli agents arrested and jailed hundreds of suspects, but Arafat was never caught. He was able to elude authorities by dressing up as an old man, a shepherd, and even a woman. He seemed to possess an uncanny ability to sense when danger was near and many times avoided capture. One time Arafat, disguised as an old man, was about to enter what was believed to be a Fatah "safe house" in East Jerusalem. Outside the house, he paused and sensing danger, left. In less than half an hour, Israeli soldiers surrounded the house, hoping to find Arafat inside.[8]

B Y THE END OF AUGUST, Fatah had staged its first terrorist attack on Israel since the Six Day War. Attacks on both army and civilian targets were intended to raise Palestinian morale by proving that the enemy was weak and establishing Fatah as a worthy adversary. But Arafat did not have an easy time at first. Besides having to move around secretly, he had to contend with the many levels of power that existed within Palestinian society in Gaza and the West Bank. For many years, wealthy Palestinian families had lived and prospered under Jordanian rule by doing business with the occupying authorities. Many assumed that the Israelis would not be that different from the Jordanians. They were not interested in supporting a grassroots political movement that would upset their position in society.

Arafat had to appeal to students who were filled with political idealism and the middle-class merchants who had nothing to lose by becoming involved. After traveling from village to village, trying to organize, Arafat was detected by Israeli agents, thanks to a Palestinian informant, and had to flee to Jordan. The experience taught Arafat that there were very few people he could trust, anywhere. He realized that for the type of action-oriented, military struggle he intended, he had to keep his own movements and plans very quiet.

Despite having to flee Palestine on several occasions between 1967 and 1970, Arafat developed an image as an underground commando operator and daredevil terrorist. He was beginning to establish himself as a leader of the Palestinians, even though his reputation was based more on unsubstantiated reports of successful terrorist victories against Israel than on actual fact. During the three years after the 1967 war, Arafat claimed that all of Fatah's military bases were in the occupied territories and that attacks were made daily. He also claimed that Israel used "napalm bombings, strafings, evictions, summary executions, plundering, brutality, imprisonment, desecration, violations and countless other crimes" against his people's armed struggle.[9] None of these claims was based on fact. This kind of propaganda helped mobilize support but ultimately gave people a false sense of Fatah's strength in Israel.

Israel was not going to stand for organized rebellion against its rule. Israeli authorities felt they had made concessions regarding the Palestinians' living in the occupied areas and were not going to be terrorized at the same time. While Fatah boasted of making great inroads into reclaiming all of Palestine, it had in fact done very little to shake the Israeli government. Barry Rubin explains, "Like so much of the movement's history, public relations' success went hand in hand with debacle. Fatah's terrorist guerrilla operations inflicted civilian and military casualties but hardly destabilized the country. Israel defeated the offensive by mounting a focused, effective repression against activists and permitting a relatively normal life for Palestinians who refrained from involvement in the insurrection."[10] Many people realized that they could lead a relatively peaceful and successful life by cooperating with the authorities.

Arafat persisted, however, in sending his commandos across the Jordan River every night to attack Israeli soldiers on the other side. When the PLO gunmen realized that they could not fight the army effectively, they chose instead to aim their guns at civilian targets. Between 1967 and 1970, Palestinian terrorists were responsible for 115 Israeli civilian deaths and for wounding another 687 nonmilitary Israeli citizens.[11]

One battle between principally Jordanian forces and invading Israeli soldiers intent on destroying the main Fatah camp at Karameh, Jordan, became a legendary Fatah victory. Actually, only a few Palestinians had participated in the fighting, in which twenty-one Israeli soldiers had died. Nevertheless, the Palestinians claimed their objectives had been achieved, and the battle took on heroic proportions. Jordan's role in the fighting was all but forgotten. Recruits poured in from the refugee camps once word had reached them that Fatah had struck back against the Israeli "imperialists."

Thanks to Fatah's popularity, President Nasser of Egypt, founder of the original PLO and chief of the Pan-Arab movement (a movement to unite all Arab countries and fight for common progress), helped Arafat take over the organization. In February 1969, Arafat became chairman of the PLO. He saw himself as a man of action whose sole aim was the liberation of Palestine: "We have no ideology—our goal is the liberation of our fatherland by any means necessary, by blood and iron; and blood and iron have nothing to do with philosophies and theories. It is the commandos who will decide the future."[12] In 1969 alone, Arafat's PLO carried out 2,432 terrorist attacks on Israel.

He now appeared always as a fighter in military uniform, armed with a pistol or a rifle. To Western eyes he was perceived as a terrorist, while his fellow Palestinians saw him as a true man of the people. In the new PLO charter, Arafat stressed that all decisions regarding the Palestinian people and cause were made by the PLO, not by an outside authority. The PLO's central goal was to eliminate Israel from every

Yasir Arafat speaks as the new chairman of the PLO in 1969. He had struggled for years to reach this position, and he would succeed in retaining control despite setbacks and fragmentation from within.

inch of Palestinian soil, regardless of the sacrifices entailed. According to Arafat, the only means possible for liberating Palestine was an armed struggle.

Arafat felt that "the PLO had priority over every other issue and a right to free use of Arab territory." But, according to Arafat, other Arab countries "did not accept the PLO's independence because the Palestine issue's very importance made it too valuable to leave in the PLO's control."[13] Regardless of the future, Arafat had already achieved what he had believed impossible only a few years earlier.

He had begun to reawaken Palestinian nationalism, garnered international attention for the PLO, firmly entrenched bases in Jordan and Lebanon from which to attack Israel, and developed an armed force strong enough to rival the armies of both Lebanon and Jordan. He had begun to create a temporary Palestinian state within these two small Arab nations and enjoyed support from leftist groups, radical nationalists, Muslims, and Palestinians. The PLO paid regular wages to its fighters, gave pensions to widows and children, set up schools, hospitals, and courts in the refugee camps, and tried to offer some 1.7 million refugees the services that any government would offer its people.

Arafat believed he was poised for victory, but in fact, his organization faced a number of major obstacles. He had not quite succeeded in uniting Palestinian forces, he did not have complete Arab support, and his use of terrorism against civilians made him loathsome and untrustworthy to the Western powers. While he claimed triumph at the beginning of the 1970s, Arafat's and the PLO's substantial opposition remained strong.

Chapter Six
The Height of Terrorism

ARAFAT AND FATAH'S popularity and guerrilla strength were at such a height in the beginning of the 1970s that Arab governments in the Middle East were forced to accept an independent PLO in their own countries. However, the relationship between Arab nations and the PLO was never a very comfortable one. While dealings with Arab countries were often strained, they were not the only sources of conflict for Arafat and Fatah, the biggest and most influential branch of the PLO. Many other Palestinian organizations sprang up during the late 1960s and early 1970s to challenge Arafat's Fatah as the sole legitimate body representing Palestinians.

While there were at least fourteen other guerrilla groups challenging Arafat, the two presenting the greatest threat were the Popular Front for the Liberation of Palestine (PFLP), led by George Habash, and the Democratic Front for the Liberation of Palestine (DFLP), led by Nayaf Hawatmeh. These groups were steeped in Marxist ideology and the desire to bring about a class revolution as well as the liberation of Palestine. They directed their actions not only at destroying Israel but also at other Arab governments that they saw as oppressive and within the influence of Western imperialists. While Arafat's main goal was regaining every inch of Palestinian soil, the PFLP and the DFLP were interested in bringing about a complete change in Arab society, where the poor would overcome their wealthy "oppressors." Like the PLO, the PFLP and the DFLP have employed terrorism as a principal means to their ends.

PLO headquarters was based in Jordan by the end of the 1960s, and Arafat felt his position was strong enough to speak out against Jordan's king Hussein, whom he considered too moderate in his approach to the Arab-Israeli conflict. Arafat's claims so greatly angered Hussein that in the fall of 1970 he declared war on Fatah and the fedayeen, or "men of sacrifice," the name Arafat had given to his fighters. Many of Arafat's men were killed in the fighting, and in 1971 the PLO was forced to move its operations to Syria and Lebanon. This was neither the first nor the last time Arafat and the PLO were forced out of a host country.

SIGNIFICANT CHANGES were taking place in the Middle East during the early 1970s that would affect events for decades to come. In 1970, Egyptian president Nasser died, and his vice president, Anwar el-Sadat, took office. While Arafat was working toward provoking another war with Israel, Sadat took the initiative on October 6, 1973, on Yom Kippur, the holiest day of the Jewish year, to launch an attack on

Israel with a combined army of Egyptian and other Arab forces. While the Israelis were caught unaware and suffered losses, in the end they were able to drive back the invading forces and lost no territory.

Even though no territory was gained during the war, Arab military pride had been restored and several factions within the Arab world consolidated to support Sadat.[1] The Israelis, having flaunted their invincibility and military superiority, now realized they were vulnerable and had to always be on their guard, even on as holy a day as Yom Kippur. While Arafat did not have anything directly to do with the Yom Kippur War, he took it as an opportunity to proclaim that the war "has given us part of Palestine, and the fifth war will give us Tel Aviv."[2] This made no sense and was clearly propaganda to raise morale for future battles, as no part of Palestine had been regained.

While Arab forces were continuing their struggle against Israel, the PLO and several splinter groups were escalating their campaign of terrorism. Terrorism for these groups had benefits and drawbacks. Although these acts of bloody violence, in the Middle East and abroad, brought the groups international attention and press coverage, abominable acts of terror also served to discredit the groups as legitimate representatives of the Palestinian people, many of whom remained poor refugees in camps or lived peacefully under Israeli rule in the occupied territories. This gap, between those fighting on the outside and those living in poverty in camps or as second-class citizens under the Israelis, would serve to splinter Arafat's support even more significantly.

While the PLO and other groups felt that terrorism directed at Israeli soldiers, civilians, and anyone who sympathized with the Israelis in other countries was their only military option, they also functioned successfully as a government for displaced Palestinians in the camps. In Lebanon, which became the PLO's base after it was expelled from Jordan, it set up schools, factories, hospitals, and many other facilities for the half million refugees confined there.

However, the PLO gained attention for its terrorist acts, not for setting up schools in refugee camps. Thomas L. Friedman writes in his work on the Middle East, *From Beirut to Jerusalem,* of terrorism and the PLO:

> Some PLO factions went to the opposite extreme, eschewing any form of conventional warfare and concentrating instead on spectacular headline-grabbing terrorist attacks or airline hijackings inside and outside Israel, augmented by occasional guerrilla shelling of Galilee. This terrorism was another form of theater. It was a means of winning attention in the television age, but it was no means for winning a war. There is no question that these spectacular operations put the Palestinian cause on the news agendas of Israel and the world at a time when the world would have been more than happy to go on ignoring the Palestinian issue. In a sense, I believe that terrorism, while morally repugnant, was functionally relevant for the PLO at its takeoff stage. The problem was that these spectacular terrorist operations became an end in themselves, instead of just a necessary phase or instrument in a larger struggle to achieve a political solution.[3]

The early 1970s witnessed barbarous acts of terrorism, which only gave way to even more horrifying events.

In May 1970, PLO guerrillas, having crossed the border from Lebanon into Israel, fired a rocket into an Israeli school bus, killing nine children and three teachers, and wounding nineteen other children. Arafat rationalized the killing of innocent civilians by saying, "Civilians or military, they're all equally guilty of wanting to destroy our people."[4]

Radical factions of the PLO, such as the PFLP and DFLP, were more active in international terrorist operations than Fatah. Beginning in 1968, with the hijacking of a Rome-Tel Aviv flight of El Al (the Israeli national airline), and continuing for the next fourteen years, Palestinian terrorists seized twenty-nine more planes, attacked airports, and planted bombs on planes.

Between 1969 and 1985, PLO groups were responsible for more than 8,000 terrorist acts, most of which took place in Israel. However, more than 650 Israelis were killed abroad in at least 435 acts of violence. Of those Israelis killed abroad, three quarters were civilians, and the hundreds of other people murdered were from various countries.[5]

While Arafat generally believed that international terrorism was ineffective in fighting directly against the enemy, he occasionally shifted from this position. One reason for this was that Fatah had been losing status among Palestinians after Jordan crushed them and kicked them out of the country. Fatah's leaders did not necessarily feel that such terrorist attacks advanced their cause but sensed that they might lose control of the PLO if they did not resort to using such dramatic methods as blowing up and seizing international airplanes.

In 1972 at the Olympic Games in Munich, West Germany (Germany was divided into West and East at the time), eight members of Black September (the terrorist faction of Arafat's Fatah group in the PLO) slipped into a dormitory and kidnapped eleven Israeli athletes. The terrorists immediately killed two of the athletes who resisted them and stated their demands by tossing a note out the window: They wanted two hundred Palestinian prisoners released from Israeli jails and a plane to fly the terrorists to an Arab country.

Israel refused to yield and asked the Germans to keep negotiating. The Germans told the terrorists they would take them and the hostages to an airport, where a jet would fly them to Egypt. At the airport, hidden German marksmen began firing and a shootout ensued. The terrorists shot the nine athletes and blew up the helicopter that held their bodies. The Germans jailed three surviving terrorists, but within weeks they were released in exchange for eleven German hostages taken when Palestinians hijacked a German airplane.

Other Black September terrorist acts included murdering Jordan's prime minister, Wasfi Tal, in November 1971, seizing the Israeli embassy in Bangkok, Thailand, hijacking a Sabena (Belgium airline) jet, and invading a Saudi Arabian embassy reception in Khartoum, Sudan, and taking several diplomats hostage. When the terrorists' demands were not met after the Saudi embassy kidnappings, the Black Septembrists killed two Americans and one Belgian hostage.

Black September had been formed when Fatah leaders handpicked 150 terrorists to participate. The

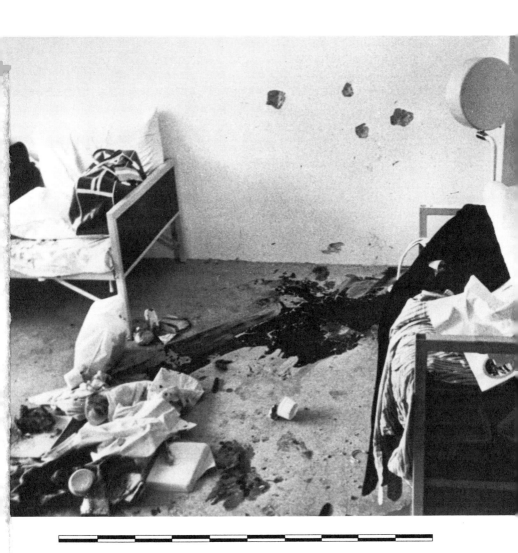

September 1972: The blood-stained, bullet-ridden apartment where two Olympic athletes were killed by Arafat's Black September terrorists. Nine other hostages were also killed. Terrorism was a tool used by the PLO to gain international attention for their cause.

group had grown to about 300 by mid-1974 and was supported by a special fund established by Arafat. Sometime after the Munich events, Arafat decided not to support Black September and told Palestinians not to participate in its raids. By late 1974, Black September was no longer an official wing of Fatah. However, two Black September terrorists, Abu Mahmoud and Abu Nidal, chose to ignore Arafat and continued committing acts of terror in the Middle East and abroad. Abu Nidal, a ruthless killer who formed his own terrorist group and aligned himself with Iraq, was responsible for orchestrating some of the most horrific terrorist acts of the last twenty-five years.

Diana Reische states in her biography of Arafat, "Most observers think Arafat tried to curb international terrorism after 1973 not because he felt any distaste for murder or kidnapping, but on practical grounds. International terrorism did nothing to get Palestine back, and turned world opinion against Palestinians in general."[6] Attacks on Israel continued, and few Palestinians regarded raids against Israelis as terrorism. To them it was a legitimate tactic for fighting the invaders of their homeland.

But no attack went without reprisals from the Israelis. After the Munich tragedy, Israeli jets bombed Palestinian refugee camps and ground commandos raided them. After 1972, Israel's security agency, the Mossad (similar to the CIA in the United States), began tracking down Palestinian terrorists and PLO leaders and killing them.

WHILE PALESTINIANS AND ISRAELIS bombed, maimed, and killed each other with increasing ferocity, Arafat was gaining status as a statesman and diplomat in international circles. He had managed to escape many attempts on his life and had ensured funds for his movement by knowing whom to appease among Arab and world leaders. He had also brought the Palestinian people and their cause to the attention of the international media. In view of these achievements, he was asked to appear before the General Assembly of the United Nations to discuss the Palestinian issue.

On November 13, 1974, wearing his battle fatigues, kaffiyeh head scarf, and an empty gun holster, Arafat stood before the General Assembly and received a standing ovation from delegates who were from countries that had won their independence through revolutionary struggle. He made his famous statement about bearing an olive branch (a symbol of peace) in one hand and a freedom fighter's gun in the other, pleading with the Assembly not to let the olive branch fall from his hand. A week after his speech, the General Assembly voted United Nations Resolution 3236, recognizing the rights of the Palestinian people to "self-determination, national independence and sovereignty." They also granted the PLO observer status at the meetings, meaning a representative could watch the proceedings at the UN but could not vote on issues.

Many who observed Arafat through the 1970s believed that the Yom Kippur War and his speech at the United Nations brought about a shift in the PLO chairman's ideas and tactics. The 1973 war had uncovered a new weapon that many Arab republics found more effective than bombs against the West—oil. The oil-producing states of the Organization of Pe-

November 1974: Arafat makes a point during his address to the United Nations General Assembly. "I have come bearing an olive branch," he said, "and a freedom fighter's gun." This speech was a turning point in legitimizing the Palestinian struggle for the homeland.

troleum Exporting Countries (OPEC) cut back on their shipments of oil to the United States and some European nations after they supported Israel during the Yom Kippur War. Oil prices skyrocketed, and the world economy was shaken to its core. Countries such as Saudi Arabia, who were more conservative in their political beliefs and actions than other Arab nations, found that they had great political control and strength by playing the oil card. They also supported the PLO and donated large sums of money from oil profits. As the OPEC nations preferred to negotiate issues along political lines rather than military ones, the PLO now found it wanted to follow suit.

By the mid-1970s, Arafat was trying to shift the political and military goals of his organization, but to many radical members of the PLO, such as the PFLP's George Habash, he had become too moderate in his approach. At the 1973 Palestine National Council meeting, Arafat attempted to explain that it was time to consider accepting Israel's existence and for the PLO to work toward a Palestine mini-state consisting of Gaza and the West Bank. He argued that too many wars had been lost and that diplomacy was a better means of attaining a homeland than warfare. The PLO now formally split into two parts, with the more radical factions forming groups that refused to compromise. They aligned themselves with Libya, Iraq, and other more hard-line Arab countries.

George Habash threatened to sabotage any international conference that tried to promote UN Resolution 242, which called for the recognition of Israel by Arab states and its right to exist. It also called for a just settlement of the Palestinian refugee problem, which did not include resettlement in Palestine. All factions of the PLO rejected Resolution 242 during the 1970s.

While Arafat spoke of using diplomatic means to gain a Palestinian homeland of some sort, his organization still carried out scores of raids against Israel between 1974 and 1980. The PLO was based in southern Lebanon and Syria during these years and had relatively easy access to Israel's borders. PLO guerrillas often crossed borders at night, attacking border settlements, ambushing Israeli patrols, and planting mines and bombs. However, all of these tactics only succeeded in angering the Israelis. Despite raid after raid, the PLO had not won back one inch of territory. While Arafat claimed he wanted to negotiate a peace settlement, he swore never to recognize Israel as a legitimate state and would not renounce terrorism. The Israelis wanted nothing to do with him and certainly did not trust the man who ordered terrorist attacks against schoolchildren and innocent civilians.

An event on the first anniversary of Arafat's United Nations speech highlighted his contradictory stance regarding terrorism and diplomacy. A 23-pound (10-kilogram) bomb, planted by Fatah, exploded in front of a coffeehouse in downtown Jerusalem, killing seven people and wounding forty. Barry Rubin relates in *Revolution Until Victory* that, "this terrorist act was a curious but appropriate symbol of PLO strategy: a massacre to celebrate a diplomatic victory."[7]

Other events were conspiring to make Arafat's life and work more difficult. The PLO had firmly entrenched itself in southern Lebanon, and its members were making themselves unwanted houseguests in a country that was suffering its own internal strife.

Civil war was brewing in Lebanon between its Christian and Muslim populations, and the flames of tension were further fanned by the PLO presence. The PLO was not directly responsible for the fighting in Lebanon but had contributed to the problems by weakening the central government's power, escalating armed conflict, arming Lebanese revolutionaries, and provoking the Christians. The PLO's very presence in southern Lebanon incited Israeli attacks over the border and angered the Lebanese Muslims who lived there. The organization also caused trouble by detaining Lebanese officials and citizens, encouraging corruption and undisciplined behavior among its forces, and refusing to remove offices and military units from residential neighborhoods after repeatedly promising to do so.

While the situation in Lebanon was heading toward a disastrous confrontation, Arafat was traveling almost daily from country to country, seeking both military and financial support. Beginning in January 1976, Lebanese Christian forces, supported by the Syrian army, surrounded the Palestinian refugee camp at Tel al-Zaatar and pounded the camp with heavy guns for several months. Arafat appealed to Egypt, Jordan, and the UN for help, but to no avail, and Tel al-Zaatar fell in August. Between January and August, an estimated four thousand Palestinians had been killed in battles. President Hafez Assad of Syria, who worried that a PLO takeover would block him from dominating Lebanon, sent in forces. By the end of 1976, Assad's troops occupied two thirds of Lebanon and put severe restrictions on the PLO.

Arafat's next blow came from Egypt. Tired of war and facing mounting economic problems, President Sadat, in a November 1977 speech, offered to go to Israel and make peace. Arafat, who had been asked by Sadat to accept UN resolution 242, responded with shock at Sadat's pledge to make peace with their mutual enemy. Sadat went ahead with his plan and visited Jerusalem, speaking to Israel's parliament and praying at the al-Aqsa mosque. In September of 1978, Egypt and Israel signed the United States-mediated peace accords. President Sadat, Israeli prime minister Menachem Begin, and U.S. president Jimmy Carter made historic handshakes in front of the White House in Washington, D.C. A peace treaty followed in March, and the normalization of relations began in August 1979. Both Sadat and Begin were awarded the Nobel Peace Prize for their efforts.

Sadat's Arab neighbors were furious, however, and the Arab League promptly expelled Egypt. Eighteen Arab countries imposed economic and political sanctions on Egypt. While this was a perfect opportunity for more radical Arab nations, such as Iraq and Syria, to band together against another common enemy, internal squabbling and jealousies only caused disunion and disorganization. Once again Arab self-interest prevented leaders from seeing the bigger picture and making any real gains. Unfortunately, Sadat would not live to witness peace in the Middle East; he was assassinated by fanatical Muslim militants in October of 1981.

In 1979 the shah of Iran was overthrown by an Islamic revolution, and the ayatollah Ruhollah Khomeini returned to Iran to take power after being in exile for fourteen years. The wave of Islamic fundamentalism, a political and religious movement spreading throughout the Middle East, was gaining ground. Islamic purists preached a Middle East free of Western imperialist influences and Jews and a return to a holy Muslim society. These extremist ideas appealed to students and the poor, who saw their futures as bleak and had nothing to lose by adhering to such a rigid belief system. What they did not realize, as many signed up for suicide bombing missions and no-win battles, was that they would rarely find total support from their governments. While many Arab countries would have liked to get rid of Western influence and Israel, the reality was that they could not survive without being somewhat involved with these two forces.

While all these forces were conspiring to alter Fatah and Arafat's destiny, an event in 1978 pushed matters to a head. In March, eight Fatah commandos hijacked an Israeli bus, and by the time the siege was over, thirty-seven people were dead—once again, most of them children. Israel invaded Lebanon in response, attacking PLO refugee camps, destroying several Lebanese villages, and killing seven hundred Palestinians. According to the PLO, more than half a million people fled their homes and headed north seeking shelter and safety. The United Nations sent a peacekeeping force, and Arafat agreed that the PLO would abide by cease-fire guidelines. In subsequent months, Arafat kept his end of the bargain and took ruthless action against Palestinian factions that tried to violate the cease-fire. The PLO had once again lost territory, but it gained many recruits as its leaders established themselves in the northern Lebanese city of Beirut.

Chapter Seven
Moral Outcast

BY THE BEGINNING OF 1980 most of the PLO's forces were concentrated in the once beautiful Lebanese coastal city of Beirut. Often referred to as the Paris of the Middle East because of its architectural beauty and rich cultural history, Beirut had been torn apart since the Lebanese civil war began in the mid-1970s.

During the civil war, the city was divided between the Christians in East Beirut and the Muslims in West Beirut, with both sides fighting for control of the entire country. Violence and unrest spread throughout Lebanon but was centered in Beirut, with Muslims killing Christians, Christians killing Muslims, Israelis killing PLO members, and PLO supporters attacking anyone they saw as an enemy to their cause.

One of the central problems with the PLO in Lebanon was that it had become too comfortable in its host country and had assumed too much power in a nation where its members were essentially refugees. Thomas Friedman says:

> As the PLO got spoiled in Beirut, it turned from an ascetic, authentic, and even courageous young guerrilla organization living primarily in the hardscrabble hills of south Lebanon and trying to lead an armed struggle against Israel, into a rich, overweight, corrupt quasi army and state, complete with bagpipe bands, silver Mercedes limousines, and brigades of deskbound revolutionaries whose paunches were as puffed out as their rhetoric. Instead of continuing to confront Israel in the only effective way possible—through painstaking, grassroots guerrilla warfare—the PLO drifted to two extremes which sapped its strength.[1]

While Israel attacked PLO strongholds in West Beirut and PLO terrorists raided northern Israeli settlements near the Lebanese and Israeli border, Arafat tried to restrain the more radical elements of his organization. He realized that true political, economic, and geographic gains could be made only if he formally renounced terrorism. Whether he was truly ready to do this by 1980 was unclear. Arafat had long been known to tell whomever he was speaking to at the time what they wanted to hear, whether he was sincere or not.

Arafat knew an unrestrained Israeli attack was not far off. The Israeli government was running out of patience with the PLO, based just across its northern border. In June 1982, terrorists shot an Israeli ambassador in London, prompting the Israeli armed forces to begin shelling Palestinian refugee camps in Lebanon. Although Arafat denied that the PLO was responsible—and in fact it was the radical terrorist Abu Nidal's Syrian-backed group that committed the act—Israel had had enough.

Israeli defense minister Ariel Sharon hoped to eliminate the PLO not only from Lebanon but from the world. He staged a three-front invasion beginning on June 6, 1982, by sending 90,000 troops into Lebanon along the Mediterranean coast, through the central mountains, and along the Syrian border. The operation, called "Peace for Galilee" (an area in northern Israel), was hindered by Syrian forces employed to drive back the Israelis. The PLO put heavy artillery around schools, hospitals, and other civilian structures in order to provoke Israelis to attack these sites; this ploy would make the Israelis look like barbarians when innocent people were harmed.

During the siege, Arafat was very active, visiting hospitals, checking on forces at the front line, and talking to troops. His two closest colleagues, al-Wazir and Khalaf, were directing military actions and rallying resistance. The PLO leaders' efforts were admirable but were nothing against the strength of the Israeli forces. Sharon was relentless and bombarded Beirut for two months until, under additional pressure from Lebanon and the United States, Arafat agreed to remove his men from Beirut.

As Arafat completed the evacuation of 14,000 soldiers from Lebanon by September 1, Libya's leader, Muammar Qadhafi, pleaded with PLO leaders to fight to the end. Arafat replied that if the Arab states had kept their promises to help the PLO, they

Arafat and an aide walk through the streets of Beirut during the Israeli seige of Lebanon. They are carrying Soviet-made assault rifles. June 1982.

would not be in such a desperate situation.[2] Arafat now had to retreat in order to salvage anything of the group he had fought for so many years to create. As thousands of Palestinians fled the country, Arafat himself went to Athens, Greece, on August 30 by ship. He had now been effectively driven out of Palestine, Jordan, and Lebanon.

Angered over the events that had essentially destroyed their country, and blaming the PLO for most of their problems, Lebanese Christian soldiers took revenge by massacring more than seven hundred Palestinian men, women, and children at the Sabra and Shatila refugee camps. The Palestinians once again suffered while being promised protection by both the United States and the PLO. The killings at Sabra and Shatila angered and frustrated many Palestinians, who felt traumatized and isolated from their leadership. There was little doubt that after Israel invaded Lebanon in 1982, the PLO was in virtual disarray. PLO leaders were then forced to rethink how to confront Israel in the future.

While there was great discussion among the ranks of the PLO over Arafat's leadership, most refugees, for whom he had always been a symbol of their longed-for home, continued to support him. He had transformed the Palestinian cause from an incidental grassroots movement to an international issue that had grabbed the world's attention. They felt that if he could only maintain PLO unity, some Palestinian land could be recovered. The complexity of Middle Eastern politics, where there were so many different factions vying for the same land and for economic and religious dominance, made Arafat's job of gaining some independence for his people an extremely

On the heels of the PLO defeat in Beirut,
Lebanese Christian soldiers, furious at the
damage to their country due to Arab-Israeli
hostilities, massacred more than seven hundred
Palestinians at nearby refugee camps.

difficult and delicate task. He had to please many different forces at the same time.

AFTER THE WAR and the massacre at the refugee camps, Arafat tried to create an image of a strong PLO that had fought bravely for two months against the invading Israelis. But, in fact, his organization was near ruin. The PLO had no office and no place for its forces to go. It was boycotted by Egypt and unwelcome in Jordan, Syria, and Lebanon. Feeling betrayed by his Arab brothers, Arafat considered moving operations to Greece but eventually decided on Tunisia, a country in northern Africa. Tunisia was a Muslim society, and its government had pledged support. Tunis, the capital of Tunisia, was headquarters to the Arab League and would make meetings with other Arab nations convenient. Tunisia's main disadvantage was its location 2,000 miles (3,200 kilometers) from Palestine and far from the Palestinians living as refugees in other Arab countries and the occupied areas. Nevertheless, PLO offices were established in Tunis by 1983.

Arafat's more moderate ideas for future dealings with Israel had angered many militant factions, and there was a series of proposed and planned attempts on his life. Even within Fatah, there was great disillusionment over corruption and incompetence within its ranks, and Arafat faced a desperate battle to maintain his leadership. Once again the PLO split, with George Habash's radical PFLP calling for all-out social revolution and creating a new powerful anti-Arafat group of radicals and terrorists backed by Syria, Iraq, and Libya. Once again all three of these Arab countries wanted to control the Palestinian organization for their own purposes and interests.

Arafat knew that he needed to begin rebuilding his forces near Palestine, even though he was exiled in Tunisia. To escape assassins' bullets and rebuild the PLO, Arafat and his loyal aides in Fatah moved constantly from location to location, rarely spending more than one night in the same place. Between 1982 and 1985, several events occurred in the PLO that made Arafat's attempts at reconstruction even more challenging. The Iran-Iraq war, which would last eight years, was diverting international attention away from the Palestinian movement; Syria's president Hafez Assad was attempting to take control of the PLO (and eventually Lebanon and Jordan) by eliminating Arafat, which fanned a revolt within Fatah; and Arafat began to negotiate with Jordan about a possible deal for joint control of Palestine.

The United States had meanwhile decided to start working toward a resolution of the Arab-Israeli conflict with U.S. president Ronald Reagan suggesting a "land for peace" settlement. Israel would withdraw from the lands it had taken over in exchange for recognition by and peace with other Arab countries. Israeli prime minister Menachem Begin rejected the proposal outright, vowing never to give an inch of occupied territory. President Assad, who was opposed to the Reagan plan, persuaded radical elements in the PLO that Arafat would be convinced to accept a deal that would deny the Palestinians their homeland. Assad sent Palestinian forces under his control in northern and eastern Lebanon, which Syria controlled, and provoked a rebellion within Fatah against Arafat.

Arafat, who had not been in Lebanon for nearly a year, had to return to reestablish his control over the organization. He would also have to agree to some of Assad's terms, and in late June traveled to Damascus to meet with Assad. Both men were unwilling to compromise, and within a week the Syrian president, in a humiliating gesture toward Arafat, banished the PLO chairman from the Syrian capital.

Arafat also met with King Hussein of Jordan to see if a deal could be worked out for joint leadership of Palestine, thus angering PLO radicals, who claimed he had sold out by negotiating with the man who had kicked them out of Jordan. The PLO executive council rejected Arafat's efforts in April 1983, and six days later an Abu Nidal terrorist killed Jordan's peace-talk representative. Despite the anger of radicals and the rejection of the executive council, two years later, on February 11, 1985, Arafat and King Hussein signed an agreement. They proposed exchanging land for peace with Israel and working with Israel to establish a Palestinian-Jordanian federation to govern the Gaza Strip and the West Bank.

Although the 1985 agreement with Jordan came to no avail, and King Hussein gave up the effort the following year, it was a step for Arafat in a more moderate direction. Arafat realized that his past path of no compromise had brought the Palestinians nothing, and he wanted something for his people. As Diana Reische notes, "This practical goal seemingly began to guide Arafat's actions. As a younger man, he acted and sounded much more radical, and he vowed to fight forever. Then a certain realism seemed to have set in. He saw time trickling out as a third generation of Palestinians was born in the crowded refugee camps."[3]

During 1985 the PLO was largely eliminated from Lebanese politics, but many Palestinians still lived in refugee camps there and were vulnerable to gangs of Christian militia. In May 1985, assaults on refugee camps in Beirut killed at least six hundred civilians and guerrillas, and thousands more were missing. All told, there were more casualties than in the 1982 massacre. By July 1985, Kuwait had decided to withdraw its economic support of the PLO, which represented millions of dollars, and Arafat found himself constrained even further by radical forces both within Fatah and without, as well as by his overall mistrust of both the United States and Israel. Arafat needed an agreement with Jordan to remain anywhere near the border of Palestine.

PLO-backed terrorist attacks continued throughout the mid-1980s. The Italian cruise ship *Achille Lauro* was hijacked off Egypt's coast, and a crippled, sixty-nine-year-old American man was killed. The United States and Israel refused to concede on any point if terrorism continued. Egyptian president Hosni Mubarak pressured Arafat to confine terrorist attacks to Israel and the occupied territories. Arafat signed a declaration in November 1985 and swore to punish the *Achille Lauro* terrorists, but ultimately he did nothing. In fact, Abu al-Abbas, a PLO executive committee member and the chief organizer of the luxury liner hijacking, was welcomed back into the PLO executive ranks by Arafat himself.

Arafat was now once again caught in the web of diplomacy versus terrorism and violence. The United States would not acknowledge his legitimacy unless he renounced terrorism everywhere. Israel, of course, wanted nothing to do with him, and several Arab countries, principally Lebanon, Syria, and Jordan, were furious at him and wanted him dead. Within the

PLO, there were so many factions that even Arafat himself became frustrated with the cycle of ineffective politics that led his organization nowhere. "I don't think he has ever been so demoralized," a friend said in 1985, or "ever in such a corner."[4] Throughout all the political upheaval and disunity within the PLO during the 1980s, the organization continued to attack Israel, and Israel continued to strike back forcefully. In 1985, Israelis bombed PLO headquarters in Tunis and even damaged the apartment where Arafat lived, but he was not home at the time.

In 1987, Kuwait put American flags on its oil tankers in the Persian Gulf and asked the United States for protection from the ongoing Iran-Iraq war. This support would have been inconceivable a few years before, but now American warships were in the Gulf. Due to the war in Iran and Iraq and the frustration inherent in the Palestinian-Israeli conflict, the Palestinian issue was largely ignored by Arab leaders during the 1980s.

In a 1987 interview, Arafat said of the situation: "We have two options: to continue in this very tough military confrontation between us and them, or to find the solution through the United Nations, and this means the international conference, to achieve a lasting and permanent solution to the Middle East crisis."[5] Feeling that he had few options, Arafat moved in a militant direction by restoring relations with two radical factions of the PLO: the PFLP and DFLP. Arafat, while not agreeing to limit his own authority within the PLO by any measure, announced at the 1987 Palestinian National Council meeting that the groups would be united until Palestine was finally liberated. Arafat had now managed to unify the more radical elements within his organization, and Kuwait and Saudi Arabia started giving the PLO money again. Arafat even had a meeting with his long estranged rival, the terrorist Abu Nidal.

Arafat was also trying to appease yet another party to gain ground for the Palestinians. Barry Rubin comments, "By the late 1980s . . . the PLO's options were to moderate its aims, cooperating with the United States and Jordan and compromising with Israel; to organize and mobilize the Palestinian people; to wage war against Israel's army; or to pursue a course of political intransigence and terrorism. Typically, the PLO would try all four approaches simultaneously."[6]

WHILE ARAFAT was reorganizing the PLO and trying to gain strength from outside Palestine, a movement was fast growing within the occupied territories that would soon gain his attention. Many of the Palestinians living in Gaza and on the West Bank under Israeli occupation felt that they understood the reality of the Israeli military and that they knew better than their exiled leaders how to handle their homeland. They had witnessed years of ineffective activity, gross corruption, and frustrating losses as well as a growing Israeli settlement population within Gaza and the West Bank. They felt it was time to act.

One symptom of impatience with the PLO was the growing number of Palestinian Islamic fundamentalists. While the middle-class and more-prosperous Palestinians in the occupied areas rallied for a more moderate position with Israel, students and the poor swore never to compromise on ideological and economic terms. The students and the lower classes felt they had received nothing from the society in which they were currently living, so they had nothing to lose by fighting.

This growing discontent in the occupied territories led to the organization of students into groups that would begin openly defying Israeli rules and regulations. At first the Israeli authorities allowed the student groups to meet, but they later closed Palestinian schools for two years because they saw the institutions as breeding grounds for these radical troublemakers. These student groups began the uprising known as the *Intifada,* which soon touched almost every West Bank and Gaza resident, Palestinian and Israeli alike. Sparked by the killing of four Palestinians by Israeli soldiers in Gaza, in response to an auto accident and subsequent rioting, the first riots of the Intifada began in December 1987. Thousands of young Palestinians began using stones as weapons against Israeli patrols, civilians, cars, and buses. Amazingly enough these stones and the youths who threw them created a dramatic turning point in the Palestinian-Israeli conflict.

The Palestinians in the territories were no longer helpless second-class citizens who had no control over their lives. By throwing stones and causing an uprising on a continual basis, they made Gaza and the West Bank nearly impossible for the Israelis to govern. As Intifada members—mostly ten- to twenty-year-old males—increased their attacks, the Israelis fought back with rubber bullets, beatings, and arrests. Despite the losses, the Intifada movement was gaining international attention and the attention of the PLO chairman.

January 1988: The Gaza Strip became the focus of hostilities, not only between Israelis and young Palestinians who led the Intifada uprising, but between moderate and radical Palestinians. The PLO could not stop this fragmentation from within.

· 105 ·

Arafat knew that the Intifada itself would not be able to overthrow Israeli rule and that its leaders would not be able to negotiate a settlement regarding Palestinian self-rule. Only the PLO could do that, and if the PLO failed the young Palestinians "waging war" in Gaza and the West Bank, Arafat was sure they would look elsewhere for leadership. He tried to gain control of the grassroots movement, but it was nearly impossible to do this while exiled in Tunisia. He diverted enormous sums of money to the movement, established underground communications networks, and provided medicine, food, and other supplies to those who fought in the territories. But despite all his efforts, Arafat and his aides were unable to gain complete control over the Intifada.

While the movement increased and grew, it slowly slipped out of Arafat's hands as other factions in the territories established control. The PLO's leadership was soon rivaled by groups such as the Islamic fundamentalist Hamas, responsible for many terrorist attacks within Israel, and hard-line leftist groups such as the PFLP. A large split developed between the radical and more moderate groups within Gaza and the West Bank. By the third year of the uprising, radical Palestinians were killing more Palestinians than Israelis, suspecting that their fellow countrymen were seeking cooperation and peace with Israel.

In 1988, at the Palestinian National Council meeting in Algeria, Arafat gave a fiery speech and read the Palestinian Declaration of Independence. At the same time he did not want to risk offending the United States and induce it to support Israel with even more arms and money. Arafat once again did not commit to anything concrete: He did not say he would recognize Israel; he did not say he wouldn't. He could not risk offending the international community, but he also could not risk splitting the PLO any further. Arafat's speech was deliberately ambiguous so he would not have to hold to any one position or party. A number of moderate delegates at the conference were frustrated because they felt that progress could only be made once the PLO agreed to recognize Israel.

Once again events turned. In December 1988, the State Department of the United States told Arafat that it would initiate a peace process with Israel if he would agree to conditions proposed by the United States. Arafat said he would, but on December 13, 1988, in Geneva, Switzerland, at a United Nations meeting, Arafat broke his promise by giving another vague speech. Realizing that he was forfeiting yet another diplomatic opportunity, he later said at a press conference: "Our desire for peace is strategic and not a temporary tactic. . . . Our state provides salvation for the Palestinians and peace for both Palestinians and Israelis." He accepted the "right of all parties concerned with the Middle East conflict to exist in peace and security, including—as I said—the State of Palestine, Israel, and other neighbors." He added, "We totally and categorically reject all forms of terrorism . . . enough is enough, enough is enough. . . . We want peace . . . we are committed to peace, and we want to live in our Palestinian state and let others live."[7] In response to Arafat's declaration of intentions, the United States was ready, for the first time, to engage in negotiations with the PLO.

However, Arafat made the grave mistake of not preparing Palestinians for the reality of the negotiations. He failed to mention that concessions would be made, implying that if they were patient, all of Palestine would be given to them. Arafat also continued to antagonize the Israeli leadership—who were reluctant and ambivalent, to say the least—by asserting that Israel was only a puppet of the United States and that all Israeli decisions were really made in Washington, D.C. But Arafat had made some progress during the December 1988 Geneva press conference, and during the same month he was received by the Pope. Later, in 1989, the European Community leadership met with him, and he was invited by France's president, François Mitterand, to Paris.

While Arafat basked in the praise of the diplomatic community, the Intifada raged on. The movement managed to annoy Israel and provoke retaliation, but lacking any real unity, it made no progress in gaining territory or independent rule. In fact, almost a thousand Palestinians were killed in demonstrations against Israeli patrols in Gaza and the West Bank between December 1987 and the end of 1990.

Arafat claimed to have gained control over the situation, whereas most Palestinians in the territories felt he really did not know what was going on at all. He became more nervous during the months of 1989 as he felt no diplomatic progress was being made with the United States. The Intifada, like the entire Palestinian movement, was becoming commonplace, and members of the international community were losing interest in it. Several other peace plans were proposed by President Mubarak of Egypt, the new U.S. president, George Bush, and even the Israeli government, which put forth a plan for Palestinian elections within the occupied territories. But none of these proposals amounted to anything. Peace efforts that had begun in 1988 and continued through 1990 were all squandered by Arafat, who could not make a firm commitment to one government, group, or practice.

In August 1990, when Iraqi dictator Saddam Hussein invaded Kuwait, intent on taking control of the country's vast economic resources, Arafat applauded his efforts. Saddam's actions, motivated by the need for money after fighting an eight-year war with Iran as well as the desire to annex Kuwait and control its oil, appalled most of the world. Arafat's decision to support Saddam proved to be a mistake, since it deprived the PLO of economic support from Kuwait and other OPEC countries while disgracing the organization throughout the world.

Chapter Eight

The Battle for Peace

O N AUGUST 2, 1990, the rest of the Arab world and Western countries looked on in horror as Iraqi tanks rolled into the thinly populated country of Kuwait. Arafat hailed the invasion as a great victory over Western imperialism and a step forward for Islam. Kuwait's royal family, which had supported the PLO for over twenty years with billions of dollars in economic aid, immediately stopped all payments.

Arafat praised Saddam Hussein while visiting the Iraqi capital of Baghdad, proclaiming through the PLO news agency WAFA to Palestinians in the West Bank and Gaza that "we can only be in the camp hostile to Israel and its imperialist allies, who have mobilized all their sophisticated war machine not to come to anybody's aid but to protect their own interests." By this statement, Arafat meant that the United States, which would become engaged in the Gulf War officially in January of 1991, was helping Kuwait only to protect its oil interests in the Middle East. According to Flora Lewis, a foreign affairs columnist for *The New York Times,* Arafat's statement from Baghdad undid "years of his own energetic diplomacy. So much for the peace initiative, the desire for negotiations, the recognition of Israel." [1]

But the United States was not the only country to act militarily against Iraq. An Arab summit meeting voted twelve to three to condemn the invasion and sent in troops from several Arab nations to defend Saudi Arabia in case of an Iraqi attack. The three Arab votes against the protection of Saudi Arabia were cast by Libya, Jordan, and the PLO. Many PLO supporters went to Baghdad to enlist in Saddam's forces, and Palestinians in the West Bank and Gaza openly cheered Iraq's invasion of Kuwait. When Saddam proposed removing his troops from Kuwait if the Israelis left the occupied territories, Palestinians saw him as a new savior. Skeptics doubted that Saddam would ever do such a thing, but the proposal was effective for gaining support for Saddam.

According to Diane Reische, "Western observers said Arafat's decision to tie himself to Saddam Hussein had cost Arafat all the momentum and goodwill gained by the Intifada, and made it impossible to talk of solving the Palestinian dilemma soon." [2] By refusing to bend on his hard-line stance regarding the Gulf War, Arafat ensured that the United States and Israel would have nothing do with him with regard to peace talks.

Once again he had proved himself untrustworthy. Arafat's behavior proved to the Israelis, who were bombarded with Iraqi missiles during the Gulf War, that the PLO could not be trusted and did not really want peace with them.

When Arafat supported Saddam Hussein (right) during the Gulf War, he angered moderate Palestinians and lost credibility with the many Arab nations that opposed the Iraqi invasion of Kuwait. The PLO became even more mired in factious infighting and debt.

While Arafat's position was popular among poor Palestinians and Islamic fundamentalists, he angered many Arab leaders and wealthy Palestinians who supported the more moderate stance he had been taking. His support of Saddam's actions came as a shock to many Palestinians who thought that he was on the verge of attempting peace with Israel. Arafat suddenly found himself without money for his organization and once again had to start furiously backpedaling to reverse his position. While the United States and an allied force of troops from Arab and European countries militarily crushed the Iraqi invaders and sent them limping out of Kuwait, Arafat called for a United Nations peacekeeping force to be employed in Kuwait once Iraqi troops had withdrawn. He tried to use this suggestion to renew peace talks with Israel and the United States. But Arafat's recent actions supporting Iraq had severely hindered his credibility.

Peace talks resumed again between Israel and Palestine, in Madrid, Spain, in October 1991, but Arafat was not there to represent his people or his organization. Instead Haydar Abd al-Shafi, the Palestinian delegation's leader, presented a speech that would begin a process toward a peace agreement. (The agreement itself, which would occur two years later, in 1993, would directly involve Arafat.) Abd al-Shafi's speech was approved by the PLO, and he mentioned his support for his leadership (the PLO), but it was he delivering these words and not Arafat.

Despite Arafat's support of Iraq during the Gulf War, a mistake he clearly regretted, he had come to realize that forty years of armed struggle, rejection of Israel, and a mass uprising of the Palestinian people (the Intifada) had not brought the Palestinians any closer to having a homeland they could call their own. Other countries surrounding Israel (Jordan, Lebanon, Syria) were more concerned about Iran and Iraq than they were about an Israeli threat and were making their own deals with Israel for land and economic possibilities. Arafat realized the time had come for him to try peace. "It is entirely impossible for the PLO to remain an onlooker because the Palestinian people will have to live with its results,"[3] claimed Arafat, regarding a possible peace conference.

In the Israeli election of June 1992, a new government came to power, which helped place the peace process back on track. Both the new prime minister, Yitzhak Rabin, and his foreign minister, Shimon Peres, were amenable to trading land for peace.

WHILE PEACE PLANS were slowly formed and negotiated, Arafat did something that surprised Palestinians, Israelis, and anyone who knew his personal life. Arafat had always maintained that he would be married to only one woman, and her name was Palestine. But in November 1991, he reportedly married a Palestinian woman named Suha Tawil (the two had actually been married on her twenty-seventh birthday in July 1990).[4] Mr. and Mrs. Arafat definitely made an unusual team. Tawil, who was thirty-four years younger than her husband and raised a Christian, was born in Jerusalem in 1963 to affluent parents. She spent her childhood in the Israeli-occupied towns of Ramallah and Nablus and was educated by French nuns. She learned to speak French, Hebrew, Arabic, and English at school and went to Paris in 1981 to study political science and linguistics. Tawil met Ara-

After the Gulf War, Arafat was forced to realize that the only path to a Palestinian homeland lay in peace. At this juncture in a life until this time devoted entirely to a militant cause, he surprised the world by marrying. He poses here with his wife, Suha Tawil, in front of a giant photograph of a Jerusalem mosque.

fat in 1985 when her mother introduced him to her during a summer holiday. They saw each other frequently during the late 1980s, but their most important meeting came in 1989 when Arafat visited her in France. Tawil says, "That was it. There were little signs before: he kept calling me on the phone, and he planted the seed, saying 'If I were younger, I would have married you.' There was a chemistry between us, it was clear. And in Paris everything came together."[5]

In October 1989, Tawil left Paris and joined Arafat's staff in Tunis. They were secretly married nine months later, but an official announcement was not made for almost two more years. Tawil became an integral part of her husband's life and work, advising him about what the PLO should do in the future. She was an independent woman, who believed in equal rights for women, liked to wear elegant French suits, and wished she did not need so many bodyguards. While Tawil converted to Islam after she and Arafat were married, she remained a practicing Christian.[6]

Tawil felt very strongly that peace between the Palestinians and Israelis was the only hope for a successful future for both countries. Her husband, she has said, "cannot walk away from it [the peace process] now—it's gone too far. And, if we stop this process now, there will be massacre after massacre. . . . But if we go ahead, then we will get the economic prize [foreign investment for Gaza and the West Bank] and the political prize will follow that. We're a tiny country, and we have no choice. We must coexist with the Israelis, and we can learn a lot from them."[7]

In April of 1992, Arafat was nearly killed in a plane crash over the Libyan desert and later, in May, had emergency surgery in Jordan to remove a blood clot in his brain. While recovering in the hospital, he suffered a stroke. Tawil was close by to comfort and nurse him back to health and to encourage him to continue working for peace between their people and the Israelis. Arafat complied with his wife and as soon as he was well enough began once again to work at the exhausting pace he had always maintained.

But there is no doubt that Arafat is getting tired. As Mary Anne Weaver described in her article on Arafat in *The New Yorker* magazine, "On the desktop . . . four bottles of pills were lined up in front of him. As I watched him massaging his eyes and the back of his neck, I thought about what a friend of his, who is one of the few surviving co-founders of his al-Fatah guerrilla movement, had said to me a few days before: 'It's been thirty years. This revolution has simply gone on too long. Then we were young; now we are old.' "[8]

After living through years of bloody conflict, Arafat, the al-Khityar (a term used by his closest associates meaning "old man"), wants to see Palestinian control of at least a piece of his homeland during his lifetime. "Guns! Guns are flowing into the territories. Those Jewish settlements [in the Occupied Territories] are powder kegs, and the Palestinian factions are arming themselves too,"[9] Arafat asserted, believing that if peace is not made between Israel and Palestine, both Jews and Arabs will suffer.

BEGINNING IN APRIL 1992, Norwegian researcher Terje Rod Larsen, who had studied conditions in the Israeli-occupied territories, offered to arrange contact between Israel's future deputy foreign minister, Yossi Beilin, and the PLO. Negotiations about a meeting advanced, thanks in part to the summer victory of the more liberal Israeli Labor party (Yossi Beilin was elected deputy foreign minister), and soon Norway offered to arrange the secret means by which Israel and the PLO could meet to begin talks. These talks would eventually lead to the signing of the peace agreement between Israel and the PLO in 1993. There were still many barriers in the way of peace (among them, Islamic and Jewish militants), but men who were sworn enemies for decades were able to lay down their weapons and attempt a settlement, thanks in large part to the coalition from Norway.

In December of 1992, initial meetings were held in London, England, between PLO and Israeli officials, who then moved to Oslo, Norway, for a series of secret meetings between January and August 1993. By the end of August an agreement had been drafted that Abu Alaa, the PLO representative in Norway, and Shimon Peres, Israel's foreign minister, found acceptable. *The New York Times* wrote on September 5, 1993: "For the first time since the Camp David agreement of 1978, the door is open to a historic Mideast peace. Once again, the breakthrough came not from Washington, but from the region itself. Then it was Anwar el-Sadat of Egypt who courageously took the first step. This time, it was Shimon Peres of Israel." Both Arafat and Israeli prime minister Yitzhak Rabin were pleased with the progress.

As usual not everyone saw the peace process as a positive step. Many Israelis could not forget Yasir Arafat, the terrorist, and did not believe that he would keep his word. Benjamin Netanyahu, chairman of the very conservative Likud party in Israel, writes, "The Rabin Government is now betting the security of Israel on Yasir Arafat's promises. But his promises are worthless. He has violated every political commitment he has ever made. Since his 'breakthrough' promise in 1988 to stop PLO terror, his own Fatah faction has launched more terrorist attacks against Israel than any other Palestinian group. Similarly, he repeatedly 'recognizes' Israel for some political gain— only to take it back later."[10] As for Palestinians, many felt that Arafat was out of touch with their concerns and for all his promises of hospitals, schools, employment, and autonomy from the Israelis, would not give them a better life or a homeland.

But with the backing of key Arab nations, such as Egypt, Jordan, and Syria, Arafat was ready by the fall of 1993 to sign the peace agreement sponsored by the United States and negotiated by the Norwegians. After being banned from the United States for almost two decades, Arafat was scheduled to meet with Israeli prime minister Rabin and U.S. president Bill Clinton on Monday morning, September 13.

After decades as enemies, the two men met and shook hands in the presence of President Clinton. The event was watched by millions around the world, including Arafat's wife, who viewed the proceedings on Cable News Network (CNN).

The agreement, so historically important and anxiously anticipated, called for Palestinian autonomy in the Gaza Strip and the West Bank town of Jericho; Israeli withdrawal of troops from those areas; and Palestinian elections within nine months of signing to create a council to oversee education, economic development, environmental protection, taxes, and social welfare. In addition, security was promised by a Palestinian police force, and hundreds of thousands of refugees were to be returned from refugee camps. There were plans for future discussions about splitting the religious capital of Jerusalem, and finally, the establishment of a joint Israel-Palestine Economic Cooperation Committee to oversee economic development in Gaza and the West Bank. Arafat stated after the signing:

> My people are hoping that this agreement, which we are signing today, marks the beginning of the end of a chapter of pain and suffering which has lasted throughout this century. My people are hoping that this agreement, which we are signing today, will usher in an age of peace, coexistence and equal rights. We are relying on your [the United States'] role, Mr. President, and on the role of all the countries which believe that without peace in the Middle East, peace in the world will not be complete.[11]

As the Israelis and the PLO worked through June 1994 toward Palestinian self-rule in Gaza and the town of Jericho, Arafat finally achieved one goal for which he had been personally striving for twenty-seven years: He returned to Palestine. Arafat communicated through intermediaries that he intended to be in the lands recently put under Palestinian authority by the first week in July. After meeting with Egyptian president Hosni Mubarak in Cairo for an official send-off, Arafat flew to an airstrip near the border of Egypt and Gaza. He then drove across the border into Gaza. Arafat arrived in the Gaza Strip, his kaffi-yeh wrapped around his head and his face characteris-tically unshaven, on Friday, July 1, after an exile of nearly three decades.

According to a *New York Times* report, "With tears in his eyes, Mr. Arafat knelt after crossing the border from Egypt and kissed the ground—land he has not seen in decades and that for the first time has come under Palestinian authority and, for now, his personal stewardship."[12] Arafat was home, and he was provisionally in charge. At the Rafah border crossing (between Egypt and Gaza), he spoke for an hour to a crowd estimated at 100,000 people. After his late-afternoon speech, Arafat wasted no time in summoning the members of his quasi government to his hotel on the beach.

Arafat's visit sent a shock throughout Israeli so-ciety, and protest groups were already beginning to block any visit he might attempt to the holy city of Jerusalem. Many Israeli citizens could not believe that their national enemy was so close to their sacred city and homeland. At the same time, Arafat appealed to all Palestinians to help him make self-rule work, which meant acknowledging Israel's existence. He wanted projects to begin immediately on new schools, hospitals, roads, bridges, building complexes, and even the promotion of tourism in Gaza. Arafat knew that none of this would be possible without fi-nancial help from the United States and other West-ern countries. If the Palestinians continued to em-brace terrorism, nothing would be accomplished. He tried to reassure Palestinians by telling them he could advocate for them abroad and also govern from within now that he had returned to the Gaza Strip.

*July 1994: Arafat kneels to kiss the ground
of the Holy Land upon his arrival in the
Gaza Strip after twenty-seven years of exile.*

Amid protests from extreme-right political parties in both Israel and Palestine, violent attacks and retaliations, and a growing militant movement in the occupied territories, Arafat flew to Jericho on July 6 for his swearing-in as the head of a new Palestine National Authority. Before the ceremony, Arafat gave a speech to an eager crowd of Palestinians, who listened to his promise that this day would be the start of a Palestinian state with Jerusalem as its capital.

Although many Israelis and Palestinians were still skeptical about the peace agreement, the general feeling in Israel, the Gaza Strip, and the West Bank was one of relief and hope for the future. That lasted until the end of February 1994.

AT DAWN on Friday, February 25, Dr. Baruch Goldstein, a U.S.-born Jewish settler in Israel, walked into a mosque (a Muslim house of worship) in the Cave of the Patriarchs (a site holy to both Jews and Muslims) in the West Bank city of Hebron and shot to death forty-three Palestinian worshipers. In a few moments, Dr. Goldstein, who was known to refer to Arabs as "Nazis" and as a "sickness in our society," [13] nearly destroyed years of planning for peace by the PLO and the Israelis. Even though Goldstein practiced medicine, he was quoted as saying, "There is a time to heal and a time to kill." [14] He was beaten to death after the massacre by Palestinians who had been praying inside the mosque.

While most Israelis did not share his views on how to resolve the Palestinian issue in Israel, Dr. Goldstein's actions announced that not every Israeli or Palestinian was ready for a peaceful resolution. In fact, since Arafat and Israeli prime minister Rabin met on the White House lawn, many extremist settlers have tried to upset further advancements of the peace process.[15] These "settlers" are Jews who have chosen to continue living in the occupied territories even though these areas are not officially part of Israel. The Hebron massacre, as it was called, began a new series of violent clashes between settlers and Palestinians in the occupied territories and in Israel proper. Many believed it also prompted terrorist attacks on Jewish centers in England and Argentina.

Although the massacre highlighted the difficulties facing those who wanted the peace agreement to take effect immediately, it was only symptomatic of other problems plaguing the process and the region. Islamic fundamentalists, specifically the terrorist group Hamas, posed an enormous ongoing threat to any current or future movements toward peace between Israel and the Palestinians. Much to their credit, after the massacre, the United States and Israel invited the PLO to continue working toward a settlement.

On February 28, three short days after the killings, a PLO official responded to the entreaties of the United States by saying, "It is too soon. The blood is still warm."[16] While Israeli government officials agreed to take severe measures against extremist settlers, Arafat dismissed the intention as "merely cosmetic." Arafat wanted tougher restrictions and promises of security if the peace talks were to continue at all. Clearly the issue of settlers in Gaza and the West Bank would be at the top of the agenda of any subsequent talks between the PLO and Israel.

The Hebron massacre did just what Baruch

Goldstein had hoped—it shocked the world. The outcry over the event made it clear that those who wanted peace still hoped for it, while those who thought peace would never work believed so even more. In other words, the two sides of the issue became even more sharply divided. Despite the fact that the massacre put intense pressure on Arafat not to resume the peace talks with Israel, on March 4 a PLO envoy, sent by Arafat, met with U.S. Secretary of State Warren Christopher to discuss the possibility of a continued effort. Arafat made it clear, through his representative, that Israel had to do more in terms of security in the occupied territories.

A week after the massacre, people expressed their anger at Arafat and the PLO for inadequately protecting them. According to *The New York Times,* by March 4 Arafat had "become one of the most reviled figures in the occupied territories," and it appeared that the massacre in Hebron had "accelerated the deterioration of support for the PLO, especially at the grass-roots level."[17] While many PLO leaders left the organization after Arafat signed the peace accord in Washington, D.C., because they were angry at the concessions the chairman had made with Israel, members abandoned the PLO in droves after the massacre.

According to Saeb Erakat, one of the chief Palestinian delegates to the peace talks with the Israelis, "People have turned against not just Chairman Arafat, but anyone associated with the peace process. . . . We promised people that things would get better and instead we have witnessed one of the worst massacres in our history. When I marched with Palestinians last September they all said we should give the negotiations a chance. Now they say that chance is finished."[18] Animosity toward Arafat was so high in the occupied territories that his posters were regularly defaced, and residents would spit or curse when asked about him, feeling betrayed by the man in whom they had once placed so much faith.

Arafat suffered an even greater blow when members of the Fatah Hawks, the military wing of Fatah, defected and began initiating violent attacks against Israelis in the occupied territories. The Fatah Hawks had brokered a deal with the Israelis after the peace accord was signed, but since the massacre had increased their attacks. The Hawks joined ranks with the Islamic militant organization Hamas, parading in the streets with the group that was vehemently opposed to any peace agreement with Israel. A leader of the Hawks stated to *New York Times* reporter Chris Hedges in March 1994: "We are all ready to renew attacks against Israeli soldiers and settlers. We have given up on the peace process and we can't stand by while Israelis massacre our people. Arafat . . . tried to make peace, but we are the ones who live here and must protect our people. We have no choice."[19]

Hamas, along with the PFLP and the DFLP, vowed to disregard any accord on Palestinian self-rule in the occupied territories if it had anything to do with Israel. All three groups considered an agreement between the PLO and Israel a betrayal to the true aspirations of the Palestinian people—the return of their homeland. They also resented the fact that Arafat still continued to appoint his close personal associates to powerful PLO positions and did not distribute responsibilities equally.

Hamas remained true to its promise, and after the Hebron massacre there were scores of violent incidents in both Israel and Gaza. A kidnapped Israeli soldier was killed, Islamic militants from Hamas bombed a bus in Tel Aviv in October 1994, killing twenty people and wounding twenty-eight more. Soon after, a suicide bomber on a bicycle blew himself up at an Israeli army checkpoint in the Gaza Strip, killing three soldiers and wounding twelve others. The Israelis were quick to retaliate after these acts of violence, further frustrating attempts at normal relations.

In light of the ongoing terror, many found it ironic that Arafat was awarded the Nobel Peace Prize in October 1994. They felt that because of Arafat's violent, terrorist past, he should never have been given the prize. To their minds, signing a piece of paper in Washington in 1993 did not erase the past, nor did it ensure that Arafat would never endorse or embrace terrorism again. While many feared that Arafat would use terrorist acts as a means to an end in the future, there were several groups of Palestinians who condemned him for not using terrorism often enough. In the Gaza Strip, Arafat's police force was often forced to contend with gangs of angry Palestinian protesters who felt that Arafat no longer spoke for them.

To many young Palestinians, Arafat's leadership had come to represent an old guard trying to control a new generation of fighters, fighters who did not agree with the chairman on many issues. One generation of Palestinians had watched as Israel signed a peace agreement with Egypt, and now a new generation witnessed a treaty with Jordan in October 1994. Militant factions only became more incensed as they saw their supposed Arab allies making peace with a

PLO chairman Yasir Arafat, Israeli foreign minister Shimon Peres, and Israeli prime minister Yitzhak Rabin display their shared Nobel Peace Prize in Oslo, Norway. December 1994.

country that was ostensibly a common enemy. There was a great power struggle between Arafat's PLO and these young militants.

By 1994 it was uncertain whether Arafat would ever fulfill his promises to the Palestinian people or would even remain their leader. Edward Said, a professor at Columbia University and former friend and advisor of Arafat's, commented on his fellow countryman in a television interview on *The Charlie Rose Show* in August 1994. Arafat, he said, is "essentially a tyrant who can't let go of any of the control. He is a fascinating figure, but he should resign now, his time has passed and he can't provide the goals we [the Palestinians] need to achieve."[20]

No one could deny, however, that Yasir Arafat had traveled far in his life and fought hard for his beliefs in the face of overwhelming adversity. From a childhood of loss and violence, to immersion in a bloody struggle for freedom, and finally to the governance of the Gaza Strip and Jericho, Arafat brought international attention to the plight of the Palestinians. By signing the historic peace accord with Israel, maintaining negotiations through the catastrophic Hebron massacre, and holding firm in the midst of Islamic fanaticism, he finally did what many of his critics thought to be impossible: He made his actions speak louder than his words.

Chronology

—■—

1917   The Balfour Declaration supports establishing a Jew-
        ish homeland in Palestine. Arafat's parents are
        married.

1922   Egypt becomes an independent state. Great Britain is
        given control of Palestine following World War I.

1929   On August 24, Yasir Arafat is born in either Cairo,
        Egypt, or Gaza, Palestine.

1939   World War II begins, and Arafat's father moves his
        family from Cairo to the Gaza Strip. Arafat's father
        volunteers him for the youth faction of the Muslim
        Brotherhood, to be trained as a guerrilla fighter.

1945   World War II ends, and the Arab League is formed
        in the Middle East.

1947   The United Nations votes to partition Palestine into
        two states: the Jewish state of Israel and the Arab
        state of Palestine.

1948   Israel is declared a state, and David Ben-Gurion becomes its first prime minister. The combined armies of Egypt, Jordan, Syria, Lebanon, and Iraq invade Israel/Palestine, intent on reclaiming all of Palestine for the Arabs. Arafat's father moves his family back to Cairo, Egypt.

1949   Israel beats back the invading forces and increases its landholdings by about one half. About 725,000 Palestinians become refugees from their homeland.

1951   Arafat begins studying at the University of Cairo.

1952   Prince Hussein is crowned king of Jordan. Arafat founds the Palestinian Student Federation at the University of Cairo. King Farouk of Egypt is overthrown by Gamal Abdel Nasser and a group of army officers.

1956   Nasser becomes president of Egypt and closes the Suez Canal.

1957   Arafat and a delegation of students attend an international student convention in Prague. Arafat moves to Kuwait to work as a civil engineer.

1959   Arafat begins publishing the newspaper *Our Palestine*.

1964   The Palestine Liberation Organization (PLO) is formed by the countries of the Arab League under Egyptian president Nasser.

1967   During the Six Day War, Israel captures Syria's Golan Heights, Jordan's West Bank, Arab-occupied Jerusalem, and the Sinai Peninsula bordering Egypt.

1969   Arafat becomes chairman of the PLO.

1970   Anwar el-Sadat becomes president of Egypt after Nasser dies.

1971   The PLO is driven out of Jordan, and Arafat sets up new headquarters in Lebanon.

1972   The Black September terrorists kidnap and kill eleven Israeli athletes at the Olympic Games in Munich.

1973   On October 6, Egypt and Syria attack Israel on Yom Kippur. The Organization of Petroleum Exporting Countries (OPEC) is formed.

1977   Menachem Begin becomes prime minister of Israel.

1978   President Jimmy Carter, Egyptian president Anwar el-Sadat, and Israeli prime minister Menachem Begin sign a peace accord.

1980   Iraq invades Iran, beginning an eight-year war between the two countries.

1981   Israel begins bombing PLO installations in Lebanon and annexes the Golan Heights. In October, Egyptian president Sadat is assassinated by Muslim extremists. Hosni Mubarak becomes president of Egypt.

1982   Israeli forces manage to expel PLO forces and headquarters from Lebanon. Arafat sails for Athens, Greece, from Lebanon.

1983   Arafat moves PLO headquarters to Tunisia.

1988   At a United Nations conference in Geneva, Arafat accepts the idea of two states—an Arab Palestine and a Jewish Israel. The Iran-Iraq war ends.

1990   Arafat marries Suha Tawil.

1993   On September 13, Arafat signs a historic peace accord
        with Israeli prime minister Yitzhak Rabin on the
        lawn of the White House in Washington, D.C.

1994   On February 25, forty-three Palestinians are massa-
        cred as they are praying in a Muslim mosque in the
        West Bank city of Hebron. Arafat returns to the Gaza
        Strip in July after nearly three decades in exile.

        On October 14, Arafat is awarded the Nobel Peace
        Prize.

        On October 20, a terrorist bomb explodes on a public
        bus in Tel Aviv, Israel.

        On October 27, Israel and Jordan sign a peace accord.

        On December 10, Arafat and Rabin accept the Nobel
        Peace Prize.

Notes

CHAPTER ONE

1. *The New York Times,* September 13, 1993, sec. A, p. 1.
2. Ibid., September 14, 1993, sec. A, p. 15.

CHAPTER TWO

1. Paul Harper, *The Arab-Israeli Conflict* (New York: The Bookwright Press, 1990), p. 8.
2. Quoted in Harper, p. 13.
3. Janet Wallach and John Wallach, *In the Eyes of the Beholder* (Rocklin, Calif.: Prima Publishing, 1992), p. 57.
4. James Haskins, *Leader of the Middle East* (Hillside, N.J.: Enslow Publishers, 1985), p. 33.
5. Quoted in Haskins, p. 34.

CHAPTER THREE

1. Diana Reische, *Arafat and the Palestine Liberation Organization* (New York: Franklin Watts, 1991), p. 36.
2. Quoted in Wallach, p. 50.
3. Quoted in Reische, pp. 37, 38.

4. Quoted in Harper, p. 19.
5. Quoted in Wallach, p. 85.
6. Ibid.
7. Ibid., pp. 89, 90.
8. Quoted in Reische, p. 42.
9. *Vanity Fair,* February 1989, p. 115.
10. Quoted in Wallach, p. 91.

CHAPTER FOUR

1. Quoted in Wallach, p. 97.
2. Ibid., p. 99.
3. Ibid., p. 103.
4. Ibid., p. 102.
5. Quoted in Reische, p. 51.
6. Quoted in Harper, p. 27.
7. Quoted in Wallach, p. 121.
8. Ibid., p. 123.

CHAPTER FIVE

1. Quoted in Reische, p. 58.
2. Barry Rubin, *Revolution Until Victory: The Politics and History of the PLO* (Cambridge, Mass.: Harvard University Press, 1994), p. 10.
3. Quoted in Rubin, p. 8.
4. Yasir Arafat, *International Documents on Palestine* (hereafter *IDOP*), May 1969, pp. 691–692.
5. Ibid.
6. Quoted in Wallach, p. 146.
7. Ibid., p. 148.
8. Quoted in Reische, p. 71.
9. Fatah Press Release, no. 1, 1968, *IDOP,* 1968, p. 305.
10. Quoted in Rubin, p. 17.
11. CIA Directorate of Intelligence, *Anti-Israel Arab Terrorist Organizations,* Special Report, October 4, 1968, Bechor, p. 8; *Lexicon Ashaf,* p. 149.
12. Arafat interviews, *IDOP,* 1968, p. 413, and 1969, p. 695.
13. *IDOP,* 1968, Harkabi, pp. 399–403; *Palestine Covenant,* p. 73.

CHAPTER SIX

1. Quoted in Haskins, p. 41.
2. Arafat's speech in Kuwait, February 20, 1974, *Journal of Palestine Studies,* vol. 3, no. 3 (Spring 1974), p. 197.
3. Thomas L. Friedman, *From Beirut to Jerusalem* (New York: Anchor Books, 1990), p. 124.
4. Oriana Fallaci, *Interview with History* (Boston: Houghton Mifflin, 1976), p. 131.
5. Ariel Merari and Shlomo Elad, *The International Dimension of Palestinian Terrorism* (Boulder, Colo.: Westview Press, 1986), p. 5.
6. Quoted in Reische, p. 90.
7. Quoted in Rubin, p. 48.

CHAPTER SEVEN

1. Quoted in Friedman, p. 123.
2. *Voice of Palestine,* July 5, 1982, and *Foreign Broadcast Information Service* (hereafter *FBIS*), July 6, 1982.
3. Quoted in Reische, p. 121.
4. David Hirst, "The Pressure on Arafat to Cross the Jordan," *Guardian,* December 19, 1985, p. 17.
5. *New York Review of Books,* June 11, 1987, p. 36.
6. Quoted in Rubin, p. 84.
7. Text, Voice of the PLO (Baghdad), December 15, 1988 (*FBIS,* December 15, 1988), p. 3, and *Washington Post,* December 15, 1988, sec. A, p. 1.

CHAPTER EIGHT

1. *The New York Times,* September 5, 1990, sec. A, p. 23.
2. Quoted in Reische, p. 156.
3. Speech in the *Middle East Reader,* June 2, 1993, p. 22.
4. From *The New Yorker,* May 16, 1994, p. 79.
5. Ibid.
6. Ibid., p. 83.
7. Ibid.
8. Ibid., p. 72.
9. Quoted in *Vanity Fair,* May 1994, p. 118.

10. Quoted in *The New York Times,* September 5, 1993, Op-Ed section, p. 11.
11. Ibid., September 14, 1993, sec. A, p. 12.
12. Ibid., July 2, 1994, sec. 1, p. 1.
13. Quoted in *The Financial Times,* February 28, 1994, p. 6.
14. Ibid.
15. Ibid.
16. Ibid., p. 1.
17. Quoted in *The New York Times,* March 5, 1994, sec. 1, p. 1.
18. Ibid.
19. Ibid., sec. 1, p. 2.
20. Quoted from *The Charlie Rose Show,* August 8, 1994.

Bibliography

─────■─────

Ben-Meir, Alon. *A Framework for Arab-Israeli Peace*. Saint Louis, Mo.: Robert Publishing Group, 1993.

Bickerton, Ian J., and Carla L. Klausner. *A Concise History of the Arab-Israeli Conflict*. Englewood, N.J.: Prentice Hall, 1991.

Bucher, Henry, Jr. *Middle East*. Guilford, Conn.: The Dushkin Publishing Group, 1984.

Connolly, Peter. *A History of the Jewish People in the Time of Jesus From Herod to the Great Masada*. New York: Peter Bedrick Books, 1983.

Fallachi, Oriana. Translated by John Shepley. *Interview with History*. Boston: Houghton Mifflin, 1976.

Friedman, Thomas L. *From Beirut to Jerusalem*. New York: Anchor Books, 1990.

Grant, Neil. *The Partition of Palestine: 1947, Jewish Triumph, British Failure, Arab Disaster*. New York: Franklin Watts, 1973.

Harper, Paul. *The Arab-Israeli Conflict*. New York: The Book-wright Press, 1990.

Hawkins, James. *Leaders of the Middle East*. Hillside, N.J.: Enslow Publishers, 1985.

Kiernan, Thomas. *Arafat: The Man and the Myth*. New York: Norton, 1976.

McDowell, David. *The Palestinians*. New York: Gloucester Press, 1986.

Messenger, Charles. Edited by Dr. John Pimlott. *Conflict in the 12th Century: The Middle East*. New York: Franklin Watts, 1988.

Pimlott, John. *Middle East: A Background to the Conflicts*. New York: Gloucester Press, 1991.

Polk, William R. *The Arab World*. Cambridge, Mass.: Harvard University Press, 1980.

Reische, Diana. *Arafat and the Palestine Liberation Organization*. New York: Franklin Watts, 1991.

Rubin, Barry. *Revolution Until Victory: The Politics and History of the PLO*. Cambridge, Mass.: Harvard University Press, 1994.

Sicherman, Harvey. *Palestinian Autonomy, Self-Government, and Peace*. Boulder, Colo.: Westview Press, 1993.

Sober, Lester A., ed. *Peace-Making in the Middle East*. New York: Facts on File, 1980.

Tessler, Mark. *A History of the Israeli-Palestinian Conflict*. Bloomington, Ind.: Indiana University Press, 1994.

Wallach, Janet, and John Wallach. *Arafat: In the Eyes of the Beholder*. Rockland, Calif.: Prima Publishing, 1992.

Index

———■———

Koran, 22, 25

Mahmoud, Abu, 84
Marx, Karl, 51
Mohammed, 15, 21-22, 26, 34
Mossad, 84
Mubarak, Hosni, 101, 108
Musa, Ahmad, 66
Muslim Brotherhood, 27, 29,
31, 42, 47, 48, 50, 54, 55

Naguib, Kamal, 47
Nahr el Bared, 57
Nasser, Gamal Abdel, 45, 46,
52-55, 64, 68, 74, 78
Nazil, queen of Egypt, 49
Nidal, Abu, 84, 94, 100, 103
Nobel Peace Prize, 14, 90

Oil, 85, 87
Olympic Games (1972), 82,
83, 84
Organization of Petroleum
Exporting Countries
(OPEC), 85, 87
Our Palestine (newspaper),
58-61

Palestine Liberation Organization (PLO)
Arafat becomes chairman
of, 14, 74, 75, 76
charter of, 65, 74
factions within, 15-16, 77-
78, 81, 87, 98, 102-103
formation of, 64
headquarters of, 78, 80

Palestine Liberation Organization (PLO) (continued)
in Jordan, 63, 73, 74, 100
in Lebanon, 88-89, 91-94,
95, 96, 100
observer status at United
Nations, 85
relations between Arab nations and, 54, 77
shifting political and military goals of, 87, 99-100
terrorist acts of, 79-82, 83,
84, 88, 91, 101
in Tunisia, 98-99
Palestinian Student Federation (PSF), 49, 50
Persian Gulf War, 15, 110, 113
Popular Front for the Liberation of Palestine (PFLP),
77-78, 81, 87, 98, 102, 106

Qaddumi, 64
Qaddhafi, Muammar, 94
Qatar, 58
al-Qudwa, Abdul Rauf, 17,
24-27, 29-31, 38, 42, 44
al-Qudwa, Fathi, 47, 56
al-Qudwa, Inam, 25, 47
al-Qudwa, Zaeed, 26

Rabin, Yitzhak, 11, 12, 13
Reagan, Ronald, 99
Refugees, 40, 41, 57, 59, 69,
71, 76, 96, 97, 100, 101
Reische, Diana, 84, 100, 111
Rubin, Barry, 63, 65, 73, 88,
103